W9-BGZ-801

JIM FOBEL'S
Casseroles

Other Books by Jim Fobel

Jim Fobel's Big Flavors

The Whole Chicken Cookbook

Jim Fobel's Diet Feasts

Jim Fobel's Old-Fashioned Baking Book

Beautiful Food

*The Big Book of Fabulous,
Fun-Filled Celebrations*

The Stencil Book

JIM FOBEL'S
Casseroles

Tasty Recipes for Everyday Living
& Casual Entertaining

by Jim Fobel

CLARKSON POTTER/PUBLISHERS
NEW YORK

**To the memory of my good friend and mentor,
James Beard**

Copyright © 1997 by Jim Fobel

All rights reserved. No part of this book may be reproduced or transmitted in any form or by any means, electronic or mechanical, including photocopying, recording, or by any information storage and retrieval system, without permission in writing from the publisher.

Published by Clarkson N. Potter, Inc., 201 East 50th Street, New York, New York 10022. Member of the Crown Publishing Group.

Random House, Inc. New York, Toronto, London, Sydney, Auckland

http://www.randomhouse.com/

CLARKSON N. POTTER, POTTER, and colophon are trademarks of Clarkson N. Potter, Inc.

Printed in the United States of America

DESIGN BY RENATO STANISIC

Library of Congress Cataloging-in-Publication Data is available upon request

ISBN 0-517-70456-0

10 9 8 7 6 5 4 3 2 1

First Edition

Contents

| Introduction |

I'm a casserole kind of guy. So I have been told. I suppose it's because I make them often and love them a lot. Casseroles have played an important role in my life for as long as I can remember.

When I was a kid in grade school, most of my favorite activities involved food. We lived in suburban Southern California during the 1950s, when bake sales, cake walks, sloppy joe fund-raisers, and backyard barbecues were the rage. But what I loved most were the PTA potluck suppers.

My mouth watered with anticipation as I eagerly awaited one of those events. I knew that my mother would contribute my favorite casserole of the day: scalloped potatoes. I also knew that there would be lasagne, beef stew, and macaroni and cheese, along with dozens of surprises. And of course, for dessert, apple crisp and peach cobbler.

Mom was always involved in the planning and organization of a covered-dish supper, so our family would be among the first to arrive on the day of the event. There would be a long table set up in the center of the room, which I loved to watch fill with food as people carried in their dishes and arranged them all around. It was like Christmas when we got to peek inside and see what they had brought. When you lifted the lid or opened the foil, delicious aromas escaped, whetting my hungry-boy appetite even more.

There would be at least three tuna-noodle casseroles to choose from and just as many lasagnes. You could expect to see baked beans, beans and weenies, candied sweet potatoes topped with miniature marshmallows, and chicken and dumplings if we were lucky. There would be a few mystery meats, chow mein hot dish, and hishy-hashy hellfire stew. And of course coleslaw, potato salad, and a Jell-O mold or two. Back then, casseroles were the most important thing going.

One of the features I liked best about those potluck suppers was that you could taste anything you wanted (and sit wherever you pleased). There was lots of laughter and plenty of talk around the tables in that noisy cafeteria, about the food, or school, or an upcoming baseball game. But there was always some gossip as well. You could hear exclamations of delight over Mrs. Forlini's favorite lasagne and critical whispers about so-and-so's sad-looking soup-burger-supper, or of the English teacher who could diagram a sentence but couldn't scramble an egg. It was all done in fun and everyone had a great time. My mom's scalloped potato casserole was always the first dish to disappear (with plenty of help from me, I might add).

Thinking back on it today, I realize that those covered-dish suppers were old-fashioned communal gatherings, a perfect way to share food with friends while visiting and making new ones. They were like sampler suppers, and everyone participated.

Although the innocent, carefree days of my childhood are gone, wonderful memories linger. I now know that those potluck suppers of yesteryear helped to educate my taste buds for the way I taste today.

As I grew and traveled more, and tasted more, America also was learning to cook "gourmet," and most of those old casserole dishes went into the closet. Let's face it, many of the concoctions had become just plain awful as busy cooks increasingly turned to convenience foods, adding a can of this and a box of that to assemble their casseroles.

But I never stopped making casseroles. I just found better and better ways of preparing them. During my travels I'd discover a tortilla casserole in the south of Mexico, or sink my teeth into the polenta of Rome; I'd find myself feasting on a giant meatball called "Lion's Head" in Hong Kong, or becoming dizzy from boozy fondue in the Swiss Alps. Wherever I went, food was my focus, and I always brought back recipes to try in my kitchen at home.

Casseroles are not an American invention. Cooks have been making casseroles from the time the first ceramic pot was thrown into the fire. We have, however, redefined the term.

What exactly is a *casserole*? My dictionary states that it is: "1. a baking dish of pottery, glass, or metal; and 2. any food, usually a mixture, cooked in such a dish." Simple. Almost anything can be called a casserole.

However, I have narrowed the definition of a casserole for this book. The vast majority of dishes here are made from ingredients that are layered or combined with a filling bland base of potatoes, pasta, or rice, so the result is a one-dish meal that you can cut or spoon into, as opposed to self-contained portions like manicotti or enchiladas. And, with one exception, there are no bones in these casseroles. That makes for easy serving and easy eating.

I find it fascinating to take the same ingredients used to make one dish, rearrange them, and create something entirely different. For example, when you layer the ingredients used to make enchiladas into a casserole, you create an Aztec pie. Or, take the ingredients for manicotti and layer them to make lasagne. When you change the arrangement, you change the structure, texture, consistency, and therefore the taste.

Another good example of this philosophy is my unstuffed cabbage casserole. I very much wanted to include a recipe for my mother's delicious stuffed cabbage rolls, but, technically, they are individual portions–little bundles of meat and rice wrapped in cabbage leaves. Then, I envisioned the ingredients separated and arranged in layers; the result is a casserole with all the flavors of Mom's stuffed cabbage made in easy, laid-back fashion. And it takes just half the time to make.

Perhaps the greatest thing about casseroles is that they taste best when made in advance so that their flavors have time to blossom. Consider freezing them, divided into portions. That way, you can fix dinner in a flash after a busy day. Not only will the dinners taste better than anything you can buy in the frozen-food section of your supermarket, they'll cost a fraction of the store price and you will know exactly what went into them. I like to make a couple of casseroles on the weekend, so there is always a good variety to choose from.

And oven-to-table casseroles aren't just for family meals; they are the perfect solution to casual, carefree entertaining. Since the cooking is completed hours ahead, you are able to relax and enjoy your own party. One of the most memorable dinners of my life was one when all I did was put out a big black bean tamale pie on the kitchen table, with a Caesar salad alongside. There was ice-cold beer and lemonade on hand, and all my friends helped themselves.

You won't find many convenience foods in my recipes. Fresh is best when it comes to flavor, so these casseroles are made from scratch. There are, however, a few high-quality canned and frozen products that I use often. At certain times of the year, frozen corn and peas can actually taste better than fresh. On the other hand, I find that frozen spinach has lost the light silken texture I love, and the flavor reminds me suspiciously of lawn clippings. Most canned tomato products are of excellent quality, and they are tremendous time-savers during preparation. But I rarely open a can of tomatoes during the summer growing season. Also, I use a can of chicken broth if there is no homemade stock in my freezer, knowing that I am sacrificing flavor for convenience.

Cheeses play important roles in many casseroles, adding protein, flavor, aroma, texture, and richness. When sprinkled between layers, cheeses melt and hold ingredients together, and when sprinkled over the top, they bubble and brown while creating everyone's favorite crusty golden brown topping. You can gain insight and learn which cheeses to substitute when in a pinch by reading the glossary on pages 181 to 190.

Because I have been cooking up casseroles all of my life, many of the recipes here are new versions of familiar ones. My mother was a simple and skillful meat-and-potatoes kind of cook, so I grew up learning the basics—from meat loaf, chicken potpie, and lasagne to pot roast or tuna and noodle. But I always wanted *more flavor* in *my* food, so I began experimenting at an early age. I soon discovered that I could add fresh basil to lasagne and make a bigger flavor, that chili peppers could spark excitement in meat loaves, and soon I was adding white wine to tuna-noodle casseroles and topping my chicken potpies with smoked bacon crusts.

During my quest for bolder flavors, I found that I could improve upon the comforting old-fashioned casseroles of my childhood. I also realized that hundreds of new ingredients had appeared in our markets since those 1950s casseroles were created. So I experimented with many of them and discovered that they gave new life to plain casseroles. After making hundreds and hundreds of casseroles while writing this book, I found out that I'm still a casserole kind of guy. In fact, I love them more than ever!

Jim Fobel

Casserole Equivalents

Here are a few tips for substituting common kitchen baking pans for casseroles:

• When you don't have the specific casserole called for in a recipe, substitute a baking pan of equal or slightly greater volume.

• In general, if you are substituting a pan that is shallower than the one specified, reduce the baking time by 25 percent. If using one that is deeper, increase the baking time by 25 percent.

• If you're uncertain about the capacity of a pan, measure water and pour it in to check.

4-CUP (1-QUART) CASSEROLES
9-inch pie plate

8-inch round pan

$7\frac{1}{2} \times 3\frac{1}{2} \times 2\frac{1}{2}$-inch loaf pan

6-inch soufflé dish

6-CUP (1½-QUART) CASSEROLES
9-inch round pan

10-inch pie plate

$8\frac{1}{2} \times 3\frac{1}{2} \times 2\frac{1}{2}$-inch loaf pan

7-inch soufflé dish

8-CUP (2-QUART) CASSEROLES
$8 \times 8 \times 2$-inch pan

$11 \times 7 \times 1\frac{1}{2}$-inch pan ($12 \times 8 \times 1\frac{1}{2}$-inch)

$9 \times 5 \times 3$-inch loaf pan

8-inch soufflé dish

10-CUP (2½-QUART) CASSEROLES
9 × 9 × 2-inch pan
11¾ × 7½ × 1¼-inch pan (12 × 8 × 1½-inch)

12-CUP (3-QUART), OR LARGER CASSEROLES
8 × 8 × 3½-inch dish
13½ × 8½ × 2-inch glass dish (12 cups)
13 × 9 × 2-inch metal pan (15 to 16 cups)
10 × 10 × 4-inch pan (20 cups)
14 × 10½ × 2½-inch roasting pan (18 to 20 cups)

| Freezing Casseroles |

If you plan ahead and want to make casseroles for the freezer, line your dish with aluminum foil and then coat the foil lightly with vegetable oil. Assemble the casserole following the instructions in the recipe. After it is assembled, cover it and freeze until solid. Remove the frozen food from the container (the foil will adhere); pack it in a sealable plastic bag or in freezer paper, and label it with the name of the dish and the date. Return to the freezer for up to about three months' storage.

To bake, place the frozen casserole back into the appropriate dish and let it defrost entirely. Bake according to specific recipes.

You can of course freeze the casseroles directly in the dishes without the foil, but then you will need more space in the freezer, and will lose the use of the dish.

Leftover individual portions of baked casseroles can be frozen too.

Chicken Potpie with a Bacon Crust

Tarragon Chicken Noodle Casserole

Chicken Basilico

Enchilada Suizas Casserole

Hobo Chicken

Kasha Casserole with Chicken Bits

| **Poultry** |

Chicken Tetrazzini

Double-Salsa Chicken Casserole

Arroz con Pollo

Turkey Ranchero Casserole

Turkey and Stuffing Casserole

Turkey Dinner in a Pot

Chicken Potpie
with a Bacon Crust

I love chicken potpies, so this deep-dish version cloaked in a rustic smoked bacon crust is a treat for me. You can start with leftover cooked chicken (or turkey) or cook a bird especially to make this, as you please. Stewing hens have the deepest chicken flavor. Make the pastry ahead so it has time to chill, and make the filling in advance so it can cool to room temperature.

MAKES: 8 servings

BAKES: At 400° F. for 45 to 55 minutes

CASSEROLE: Choose a 13 × 9 × 2-inch casserole

1 recipe Smoked Bacon Pastry (recipe follows)

12 ounces red-skinned potatoes (3 medium), peeled and cut into ½-inch dice

4 carrots, peeled and cut into ¼-inch slices

1 package (10 ounces) frozen tiny peas

3 cups diced (½ inch) cooked chicken

¼ cup chopped fresh parsley

4 tablespoons unsalted butter

1 onion, chopped

1 large garlic clove, minced

½ cup all-purpose flour

3½ cups chicken stock or canned broth

⅓ cup dry sherry

2 tablespoons cornstarch

½ teaspoon dried tarragon, thyme, or oregano, crumbled

¼ teaspoon freshly grated nutmeg

1 teaspoon salt

⅛ teaspoon black pepper

1 tablespoon fresh lemon juice

1 egg yolk, for glaze (optional)

1. Make the Smoked Bacon Pastry in advance so it can chill before rolling out (up to a day or two ahead).

2. Bring a large pot of lightly salted water to a boil over high heat. Drop in the potatoes and carrots and cover until the boil returns. Boil for 2 minutes; drain. Turn the vegetables into a large bowl, add the frozen peas, and toss (the peas will thaw and cool the vegetables slightly at the same time). Add the diced chicken and parsley.

3. Melt the butter in a large saucepan over moderate heat. Add the onion and sauté to soften, 3 to 5 minutes. Add the garlic and cook for 1 minute longer. Stir in the flour and cook for 2 minutes; the mixture will be dry. Pour in the chicken stock and stir or whisk constantly until it comes to a simmer.

4. In a small bowl, combine the sherry and cornstarch and stir to dissolve. Pour into the sauce and stir constantly until slightly thickened, 1 to 2 minutes. Add the tarragon, nutmeg, salt, and pepper. Remove from the heat and stir in the lemon juice. Pour the mixture over the chicken and vegetables and stir to combine. Turn into the casserole and stir occasionally until cooled to room temperature.

5. Preheat the oven.

6. On a lightly floured surface, roll out the pastry into a rectangle about 14 × 10 inches or slightly larger. Carefully pick up and transfer the pastry to the top of the pie filling. Roll the edge of the pastry to fit the pan and flute decoratively against the sides of the pan. In a cup, stir together egg yolk and ½ teaspoon water. Brush the glaze over the top of the pastry but not the fluted edge. Cut 4 to 5 steam holes in 3 places across the top. Place on a sheet of aluminum foil to catch any drips and bake for 45 to 55 minutes, or until the crust is golden brown and the filling is bubbly. Let stand for at least 10 minutes before serving.

Variations: Use leftover cooked turkey in place of the chicken. If white meat is your delight, poach a couple of chicken breasts in canned chicken broth; this technique will add fresh flavor to the broth (2 cans will do the trick).

Consider making two 8-inch square potpies. Bake one and freeze one (unbaked). Then bake the frozen one, adding about 30 minutes to the baking time.

Reheat: If the pie is at room temperature, bake at 350° F. for 30 to 40 minutes, until hot; if cold, add about 15 minutes.

| Smoked Bacon Pastry |

MAKES: Enough for one 13 × 9-inch casserole or two 8-inch squares

8 slices (about 6 ounces) smoked bacon, chopped or cut into ½-inch squares

2 cups all-purpose flour

¼ teaspoon salt

½ cup shortening

2 tablespoons cold unsalted butter, thinly sliced

5 to 6 tablespoons ice water

1. Place a large, heavy skillet over moderate heat. Add the bacon and cook, stirring frequently, until crisp and golden brown. Remove with a slotted spoon and let drain on paper towels.

2. In a large bowl, blend the flour and salt. With a pastry blender or 2 knives, cut in the shortening and butter until the mixture resembles coarse meal.

3. Sprinkle on 3 tablespoons of the ice water and add the bacon; stir with a fork to moisten. Sprinkle on 2 tablespoons more ice water and stir briefly. If dry, add the remaining 1 tablespoon ice water and stir just to combine. Do not handle the dough too much or it will be tough. Pat the dough into a 5 × 8-inch rectangle and wrap in waxed paper. Chill for at least 1 hour before rolling out.

Tarragon Chicken Noodle Casserole

The seductive and satisfying flavor of tarragon reminds me of light anise with a hint of clover and pepper, yet it has its very own flavor and personality. This creamy noodle casserole with spinach and chicken tastes even better when reheated.

MAKES: 4 servings

BAKES: At 375° F. for 35 to 40 minutes

CASSEROLE: Butter or oil a shallow 2-quart casserole

1 large (1½-pound) whole or split chicken breast

1 cup water

½ cup dry white wine

2 bay leaves

2 large garlic cloves, 1 sliced and 1 minced

1 tablespoon unsalted butter

1 onion, chopped

1 pound fresh spinach, or 1 package (10 ounces) frozen spinach, thawed

1 carton (15 ounces) ricotta cheese

⅓ cup half-and-half or milk

2 tablespoons chopped fresh tarragon, or ¾ teaspoon dried

1½ tablespoons fresh lemon juice

1¼ teaspoons salt

¼ teaspoon black pepper

⅛ teaspoon freshly grated nutmeg

⅔ cup freshly grated Parmesan cheese

8 ounces wide or medium dried egg noodles

1. Place the chicken breast in a nonreactive medium saucepan and add the water and the wine. Toss in the bay leaves and sliced garlic. Partially cover and simmer over low heat until the chicken is cooked to the bone, about 25 minutes for split breasts or 35 minutes for a whole breast.

2. Remove the chicken from the broth and set aside until cool enough to handle. Boil the broth over high heat until it reduces to ½ cup, about 10 minutes. Strain, then spoon off the fat, or blot off with a paper towel. You will need ⅓ cup strong broth for this recipe.

3. Melt the butter in a medium skillet over moderate heat. Add the onion and sauté to soften and lightly brown, 4 to 5 minutes. If dry, add 1 tablespoon water and let it boil away. Add the minced garlic and cook for 30 seconds longer.

4. Rinse the fresh spinach well to remove any grit. Pluck off and discard any thick or tough stems. Put the spinach in a nonreactive large skillet, cover, and cook over high heat, stirring once or twice, until wilted down, 3 to 4 minutes. Drain in a sieve, pressing to extract any excess liquid. Chop the spinach. If starting with frozen spinach, simply drain well and chop.

5. Preheat the oven, and prepare the casserole. Bring a large pot of lightly salted water to a boil over high heat.

6. In a large bowl, stir together the ricotta and half-and-half. Add the tarragon, lemon juice, salt, pepper, and nutmeg. Stir in the ⅓ cup strong chicken broth and ½ cup of the grated Parmesan.

7. Remove the skin and bones from the chicken and discard. Tear the meat into ½-inch-wide shreds, and add them to the ricotta mixture.

8. Drop the noodles into the boiling water and stir until the boil resumes. Cook, stirring frequently, until tender but firm to the bite, 6 to 8 minutes. Drain in a colander.

9. Add the noddles to the ricotta mixture, and stir to combine. Turn into the prepared casserole and sprinkle with the remaining Parmesan. Bake for 35 to 40 minutes, until well browned. Serve hot.

Variations: Start with 12 ounces of cooked chicken or turkey, torn into shreds, and ⅓ cup strong chicken stock or condensed broth. Substitute ½ cup chopped fresh basil or 2 tablespoons snipped fresh dill for the fresh tarragon. Try low-fat ricotta instead of whole-milk ricotta.

Reheat: Cover the casserole with aluminum foil. If at room temperature, bake at 350° F. for about 45 minutes; if cold, add about 15 minutes.

Chicken Basilico

Well-browned chicken and fragrant fresh basil make a lovely combination with rice. This casserole will taste best if made an hour or two before serving, so the flavors have time to blossom to their fullest.

MAKES: 6 servings

BAKES: At 350° F. for about 30 minutes

CASSEROLE: Choose a nonreactive 3-quart flameproof casserole (such as an enameled cast-iron dutch oven)

1 pound skinless and boneless chicken thighs, cut into 1-inch chunks (buy 2 pounds if skinning and boning at home)

½ pound skinless and boneless chicken breast, cut into 1-inch chunks

3 tablespoons vegetable oil

1 large onion, coarsely chopped

1 large red bell pepper, trimmed and cut into 1-inch squares

1 large garlic clove, minced or crushed through a press

1½ cups long-grain white rice

2 cups chicken stock or canned broth

1 can (28 ounces) whole tomatoes, drained, halved, seeded, and coarsely chopped to yield 1½ cups well-drained pieces

¼ cup dry white wine

1 teaspoon dried oregano, crumbled

1½ teaspoons salt

¼ teaspoon black pepper

1 cup chopped fresh basil

1. Preheat the oven.

2. Pat all of the chicken pieces dry with paper towels. Spoon 1 tablespoon of the vegetable oil into a large, heavy skillet set over moderately high heat. When very hot, add half of the chicken in a single layer, leaving space between. Brown very well on one side, 4 to 5 minutes. Turn with tongs and brown the other side for about 2 minutes longer. Remove and reserve. Add 1 tablespoon more oil and brown the remaining chicken pieces. Remove the chicken and set aside.

3. Add the onion and bell pepper to the hot skillet and sauté over moderate heat to soften, 3 to 5 minutes. If the pan is dry, add 1 to 2 tablespoons water. Add the garlic and cook for 1 minute longer.

4. Spoon the remaining 1 tablespoon oil into the casserole set over moderate heat. Add the rice and stir until golden brown, 4 to 5 minutes. Pour in the chicken stock, tomatoes, wine, oregano, salt, and pepper; bring to a boil over high heat. Reduce the heat to moderate and boil, uncovered, until most of the liquid is absorbed, about 10 minutes.

5. Add the chicken to the casserole and toss; remove from heat. Cover and bake until the liquid has been absorbed and the rice is tender, about 30 minutes.

6. Remove the casserole from the oven, uncover, and fold in the fresh basil. Let stand for at least 15 minutes or preferably longer, before serving.

Variations: Use chopped fresh cilantro in place of the basil and use 1 teaspoon ground cumin along with the oregano. For more flavor, roast and peel the bell pepper before adding.

Reheat: Cover the casserole. If at room temperature, bake at 325° F. for 25 to 30 minutes; if cold, bake for about 15 minutes longer.

| Enchilada Suizas Casserole |

This is an Americanized version of the famous Mexican dish of cream-and cheese-filled enchiladas. The ingredients seemed perfect for layering into a casserole, so I did some experimenting and came up with this substantial version. Whereas enchiladas are usually made just before serving, this casserole can be prepared well ahead of time. Serve with sliced tomatoes.

MAKES: 6 to 8 servings
BAKES: At 400° F. for about 20 minutes
CASSEROLE: Lightly oil a 13 × 9 × 2-inch casserole

1½ pounds skinless and boneless chicken breast halves, or 3 cups shredded cooked chicken

1 cup water

1 cup sliced whole scallions (8 medium)

½ cup chopped cilantro

3 tablespoons fresh lime juice

1 teaspoon salt

¼ teaspoon black pepper

18 corn tortillas (about 1½ pounds)

1½ to 2 tablespoons vegetable oil

1½ tablespoons unsalted butter or olive oil

1 large onion, finely chopped

2 large garlic cloves, minced or crushed through a press

1 fresh jalapeño chili, finely chopped with the seeds (optional)

1 tablespoon chili powder

2 teaspoons ground cumin

1 teaspoon dried oregano, crumbled

3 cans (4 ounces each) chopped peeled mild green chilies

½ cup all-purpose flour

2 cups half-and-half

1 cup chicken stock (reserved from poaching the chicken) or canned broth

1½ cups coarsely grated Monterey Jack cheese (6 ounces)

1½ cups coarsely grated cheddar cheese (6 ounces)

1. Place the chicken and water in a medium saucepan. Cover and simmer over low heat, turning occasionally, until cooked through, about 15 minutes. Remove the chicken and set aside to cool. Measure the broth; add water, if necessary, to make 1 cup.

2. When the chicken is cool, shred it. Place in a bowl; add the scallions, cilantro, lime juice, ½ teaspoon of the salt, and the pepper; toss well and reserve.

3. Working on a small plate with 1 tortilla at a time, very lightly brush both sides with vegetable oil, stacking them, until all are coated.

4. Preheat a nonstick skillet or griddle over moderately high heat. Cut 5 paper towels into quarters. One at a time (or more if your skillet or griddle is large), soften the tortillas by heating for about 1 minute, turning with tongs several times; they can lightly brown but do not allow them to become stiff. Stack between the sheets of paper towel. Peel the paper towels from the tortillas. Stack the tortillas and cut in quarters. (The tortillas and chicken can be prepared hours ahead, covered, and stored in the refrigerator.)

5. Preheat the oven, and prepare the casserole.

6. Melt the butter in a medium saucepan over moderate heat. Add the onion and sauté to soften, 3 to 5 minutes. Add the garlic, jalapeño, chili powder, cumin, oregano, and ½ teaspoon salt; cook for 1 minute longer. Drain the chilies and add them.

7. In a large bowl, stir the flour with a whisk as you pour in the half-and-half in a steady stream. Add to the saucepan along with the 1 cup chicken stock. Bring to a simmer, stirring constantly over moderate heat. Lower the heat and simmer until thickened, 4 to 5 minutes. Remove from the heat.

8. In a bowl, toss the Monterey Jack and cheddar cheeses together. Spread ½ cup of the chili sauce in the prepared casserole. Arrange one-third of the tortilla quarters (24 pieces), overlapping slightly, to cover the bottom. Add half of the chicken mixture in an even layer, and scatter with one-third of the cheese. Spoon on one-third of the chili sauce. Repeat the layering, topping with the remaining sauce (one-third of the total) and the remaining cheese (4 ounces).

9. Bake in the upper third of the oven for about 20 minutes, or until deep golden brown on top and bubbly around the edges. Let stand for 10 minutes before serving.

Variations: For more flavor, start with 1½ pounds fresh poblano chilies instead of the canned chilies; roast, peel, and chop according to the instructions on page 135.

Reheat: If at room temperature, add ¼ cup water, cover with aluminum foil, and bake at 350° F. for 30 to 40 minutes. If cold, bake 10 to 15 minutes longer.

| Hobo Chicken |

This is one of those casseroles that was born out of necessity one day when I had to cook something from ingredients on hand. I had a chicken in the freezer, potatoes in the pantry, and a bottle of beer in the fridge. Be sure to check out the variations, because you can add just about anything you want.

MAKES: 4 servings

BAKES: At 350° F. for about 30 minutes

CASSEROLE: Choose a 4-quart flameproof casserole or enameled cast-iron dutch oven

3 to 4 pounds chicken pieces, or 1½ pounds skinless and boneless chicken thighs, quartered

4 tablespoons olive or vegetable oil

2 pounds all-purpose or red-skinned potatoes (8 medium), scrubbed or peeled and cut into 1-inch cubes

4 onions, quartered

2 large garlic cloves, minced or crushed through a press

1½ teaspoons mixed dried herbs, such as oregano and rosemary

1 bottle (12 ounces) beer

2 tablespoons fresh lemon juice or cider vinegar

1 teaspoon salt

¼ teaspoon black pepper

2 tablespoons chopped fresh parsley (optional)

1. Preheat the oven. Pat the chicken pieces dry with paper towels. Cut the breast halves crosswise in half.

2. Spoon 2 tablespoons of the oil into the casserole set over moderately high heat. Add the potatoes and cook, tossing occasionally, until deep golden brown, about 10 minutes. Lower the heat to moderate and add 1 tablespoon more oil. Add the onions and sauté to soften, about 5 minutes. If dry, add 1 to 2 tablespoons water. Add the garlic and herbs, and cook for 1 minute longer. Turn out into a large bowl and reserve.

3. Return the casserole to moderately high heat and spoon in the remaining 1 tablespoon oil. Place half of the chicken, skin sides down, in the oil and brown very well, about 5 minutes (use a splatter screen if available, otherwise brown uncovered). Turn the pieces and brown for 3 to 4 minutes longer. Take out and reserve. Brown the remaining chicken in the oil that remains in the pan.

4. Pour the beer into the casserole and deglaze over high heat for 2 minutes. Return all of the chicken, except the breast pieces, to the pan. Add the potatoes and onions, the lemon juice, salt, and pepper; cover and simmer for 10 minutes.

5. Add the breast pieces to the casserole. Cover and bake for about 30 minutes, or until the potatoes are tender and the chicken is cooked. Let stand for 10 minutes before serving. Sprinkle with the parsley and serve hot, with crusty bread.

Variations: Add 2 sliced carrots and a peeled diced white or yellow turnip with the potatoes. Sauté ½ pound of quartered mushrooms with the onions. Sliced celery, artichoke heart, even black olives can be added. Crisp-cooked bacon can be added for flavor dimension. Substitute 1 cup of white wine for the beer.

Reheat: Cover the casserole. If at room temperature, bake at 350° F. about 30 minutes; if cold, add about 15 minutes.

Kasha Casserole with Chicken Bits

When buckwheat groats are roasted they become kasha, the grain with the biggest flavor of all, and one that I find totally addictive. In reality, kasha is not a grain at all but the seeds of a flowering plant and a distant cousin to rhubarb! It is a good source of complex carbohydrate and has 20 percent more fiber than oats. It is also one of the best plant sources of protein.

MAKES: 4 servings

BAKES: At 325° F. for about 25 minutes

CASSEROLE: Lightly oil an 8-inch square casserole

½ ounce dried porcini, cèpes, or other black European mushrooms

⅔ cup hot water

2 tablespoons olive oil

6 ounces skinless and boneless chicken thighs, cut into ½-inch cubes (1½ cups)

8 ounces fresh mushrooms, sliced

3 tablespoons brandy

1 tablespoon unsalted butter

1 cup diced carrot

1 cup diced celery

1 onion, chopped

1 large garlic clove, minced or crushed through a press

½ teaspoon dried thyme, crumbled

½ teaspoon celery seeds

½ teaspoon salt

¼ teaspoon freshly grated nutmeg

⅛ teaspoon black pepper

1½ cups chicken stock or canned broth

1 cup coarse-grain kasha

1 large egg

¼ cup chopped fresh parsley

1. Put the dried porcini in a small bowl and add the hot water. Let soak 30 to 60 minutes, until soft. Drain, reserving the liquid. Finely chop the porcini; strain the liquid into a measuring cup.

2. Place a large, heavy skillet over high heat. Spoon in 1 tablespoon of the olive oil and add the chicken. Stir once, and then let brown very well without stirring, about 3 minutes. Stir and cook for 1 minute. Take out with a slotted spoon and reserve.

3. Add the fresh mushrooms to the skillet and brown, without stirring, for about 2 minutes, until they release their juices. Averting your face and tilting the skillet away from you, add the brandy, and ignite it. Shake the pan for a moment until the flames subside, turn out over the chicken.

4. Preheat the oven, and prepare the casserole.

5. Place the skillet over moderate heat and spoon in the remaining 1 table-spoon olive oil and the butter. Add the carrot, celery, and onion and sauté to soften, stirring occasionally, about 5 minutes. Add the garlic, thyme, celery seeds, salt, nutmeg, and pepper; cook for 1 minute longer. Pour in the chicken stock and ½ cup of the strained porcini soaking liquid; bring to a simmer. Remove from the heat and add the chopped porcini.

6. In a medium bowl, stir together the kasha and egg until each grain is coated.

7. Place a heavy, medium-size dry saucepan over moderate heat. Add the kasha mixture and stir until toasted and fragrant, about 3 minutes. Pour in the vegetable mixture and add the mushrooms and chicken. Bring to a boil, uncov-ered, and boil over moderately high heat until the liquid is almost absorbed, about 5 minutes.

8. Stir in the parsley and turn into the prepared casserole. Cover with alu-minum foil, and bake for about 25 minutes or until very hot. Let stand for 5 minutes. Fluff with a fork and serve hot.

Variations: For a vegetarian version, omit the chicken and replace the chicken stock with vegetable stock. The porcini can be omitted entirely.

Reheat: If the casserole is at room temperature, cover with foil and reheat at 350° F. for about 20 minutes; if cold, bake about 15 minutes longer.

| Chicken Tetrazzini |

Named for the famous Italian opera singer during the dawn of this century, this old-fashioned spaghetti casserole is a great dish to make when you have leftover cooked chicken or turkey.

MAKES: 4 servings

BAKES: At 425° F. for about 20 minutes

CASSEROLE: Oil or butter a shallow 2-quart casserole

2 tablespoons unsalted butter

1 tablespoon olive oil

1 medium onion, chopped

1 large garlic clove, minced or crushed through a press

1 teaspoon dried oregano, crumbled

½ teaspoon dried basil, crumbled

8 ounces fresh mushrooms, thinly sliced

¼ cup all-purpose flour

1¾ cups chicken stock or canned broth

½ cup light cream

¼ cup dry sherry

½ teaspoon salt

⅛ teaspoon black pepper

⅛ teaspoon cayenne pepper (optional)

2 cups shredded cooked chicken (8 ounces)

½ cup freshly grated Parmesan cheese (2 ounces)

8 ounces thin spaghetti, broken in half

¼ cup plain dry bread crumbs

1. Bring a large pot of lightly salted water to a boil over high heat. Adjust an oven shelf to the top third of the oven and preheat the oven. Prepare the casserole or baking dish.

2. Meanwhile, combine 1 tablespoon of the butter with the olive oil in a large, heavy skillet and place over moderate heat. Add the onion and sauté to soften, about 3 minutes. Add the garlic, oregano, and basil; cook for 1 minute longer. Toss in the mushrooms and cook until softened, 2 to 3 minutes longer. Sprinkle on the flour and stir to moisten. The mixture will be dry, but it is best to use as little fat as possible.

3. Pour in the stock, cream, and sherry. Cook, stirring constantly, until lightly thickened and simmering. Add the salt, pepper, cayenne, and chicken; cook until the chicken is heated through. Remove from the heat and stir in ¼ cup of the Parmesan cheese.

4. When the water comes to a full boil, add the spaghetti and stir constantly until the boil resumes. Cook, stirring frequently thereafter, until the pasta is tender but just slightly firm to the bite, 10 to 12 minutes. Drain well.

5. Add the pasta to the sauce and toss to mix. Turn into the prepared casserole. Melt the remaining 1 tablespoon butter in a small skillet over moderate heat. Remove from the heat and add the bread crumbs, tossing to moisten. Add the remaining ¼ cup Parmesan and toss. Quickly sprinkle the crumb mixture over the top of the casserole. Bake for 20 minutes, or until deep golden brown on top and bubbly around the edges.

Variations: Leftover turkey can replace the chicken and linguini can replace the spaghetti. Romano may be used in place of Parmesan and you can use canned sliced mushrooms, well drained, in place of the fresh. Add ¼ cup chopped parsley for flavor and color or ¼ cup slivered fresh basil to add flavor and fragrance.

Reheat: Sprinkle the casserole with about 2 tablespoons of water and cover with aluminum foil. If at room temperature, bake at 350° F. for about 20 minutes. Uncover and bake in the top third of the oven at 400° F. for about 10 minutes to recrisp the top. If cold, bake at 350° F. 10 minutes longer.

Double-Salsa Chicken Casserole

This is make-ahead fiesta food at its finest. Although substantial and satisfying, this casserole is not overpowering or heavy because I lightly brush the corn tortillas with oil rather than fry them. By the way, don't use those extra-thin corn tortillas that are best suited for crispy flautas; instead, use sturdy ones, such as stone-ground; 1½ dozen should weigh 1¼ pounds.

MAKES: 8 servings
BAKES: At 350° F. for 40 to 45 minutes
CASSEROLE: Lightly oil a 13 × 9 × 2-inch casserole

1 recipe Fresh Tomato Salsa (recipe follows)

1 recipe Salsa Verde (recipe follows)

1½ pounds skinless and boneless chicken breast halves (4 large)

2 cups chicken stock or canned broth

2 large garlic cloves, minced or crushed through a press

½ teaspoon dried oregano, crumbled

½ teaspoon ground cumin

½ cup chopped cilantro

½ cup sliced whole scallions

18 corn tortillas (1¼ pounds)

2 tablespoons vegetable oil

2 tablespoons unsalted butter or olive oil

¼ cup all-purpose flour

1 tablespoon chili powder

½ teaspoon salt

2 cups fresh or frozen corn kernels

1½ cups shredded Monterey Jack cheese (6 ounces)

1½ cups shredded cheddar cheese (6 ounces)

½ cup canned tomato sauce

1 cup sour cream, for serving (optional)

1. Prepare the Fresh Tomato Salsa and the Salsa Verde ahead of time.
2. Put the chicken breasts in a large, heavy saucepan and pour in the stock. Add the garlic, oregano, and cumin and bring to a simmer over moderate heat. Cover and simmer gently over low heat until cooked through, 15 to 20 minutes. Remove the chicken and set aside until cool enough to handle. Reserve

the enriched broth, adding a little water if necessary to make 2 cups.

3. Tear the chicken into ½-inch-wide shreds. In a large bowl, toss together the chicken, cilantro, and scallions. If making ahead, cover and refrigerate.

4. Working on a plate, very lightly brush both sides of each corn tortilla with a little vegetable oil, stacking them as you work. Place a nonstick griddle or large skillet over moderately high heat. Soften the tortillas by turning them several times on the hot surface until lightly speckled brown. Again, stack them as they are softened.

5. Preheat the oven, and prepare the casserole.

6. Melt the butter in a medium saucepan over moderate heat. Stir in the flour and cook for 1 minute; the mixture will be dry. Add the chili powder and salt, and cook for 30 seconds more. Pour in the 2 cups reserved broth and stir as it comes to a simmer. Cook, stirring frequently, for 2 or 3 minutes. Measure out ½ cup for the top and pour the remainder over the chicken filling.

7. Place a stack of 6 tortillas on a cutting board and quarter them. Arrange them in an even layer in the casserole. Spoon ½ cup of the Salsa Verde over the tortillas and add half of the chicken filling. Sprinkle with 1 cup of the corn kernels. Combine the cheeses and sprinkle 1 cup of the mixture on top. Repeat the layering once more, and then top with the remaining 6 tortillas, cut up as before. Spoon the reserved ½ cup chicken sauce and the remaining ½ cup Salsa Verde over the tortillas; sprinkle with the remaining 1 cup grated cheese. Spoon the tomato sauce in diagonal lines over the top.

8. Bake, uncovered, until bubbly around the edges and browned on top, 40 to 45 minutes. Let stand for at least 10 minutes before serving. Cut into squares and serve hot, topped with the Fresh Tomato Salsa to taste and 2 tablespoons of the sour cream.

Variations: Use leftover roasted turkey in place of the poached chicken, omitting the poaching step but adding the seasonings to the broth. Or, use lean ground beef in place of the chicken, and sauté it to lightly brown. Sliced black olives can be added to the layers or whole black olives can be used to garnish.

Reheat: Sprinkle the casserole with about ¼ cup of water and cover with aluminum foil. If at room temperature, bake at 350° F. for about 45 minutes; if cold, add about 15 minutes.

Fresh Tomato Salsa

MAKES: About 3 cups

3 cups diced (½ inch) fresh
  tomatoes (about 1½ pounds)
½ cup canned tomato sauce
½ cup sliced whole scallions
½ cup chopped cilantro

1 fresh jalapeño chili,
  quartered lengthwise,
  partially seeded, and
  minced
1 teaspoon salt

Combine all of the ingredients in a medium bowl. If making more than a couple hours ahead, cover and refrigerate. Let return to room temperature before serving.

Salsa Verde

MAKES: About 1½ cups

½ pound fresh tomatillos (6
  large or 12 small), or 1 can
  (13 ounces) tomatillos
1 cup water
1 tablespoon olive oil

1 fresh jalapeño chili,
  quartered lengthwise,
  partially seeded, and minced
1 large garlic clove, minced or
  crushed through a press
½ teaspoon salt

1. Remove and discard the husks from the fresh tomatillos. Rinse well and cut in half. Combine the tomatillos and water in a nonreactive medium saucepan over moderate heat. Bring to a boil. Lower the heat and simmer until very soft, about 10 minutes; do not drain. Pour the mixture into a food processor or blender. If using canned tomatillos, simply drain and place in a food processor or blender.
2. Spoon the olive oil into a small skillet or saucepan and place over low heat. Add the jalapeño and garlic and cook gently for about 1 minute. Add to the tomatillos along with the salt. Puree. Cover and refrigerate if making ahead.

Variations: Add ¼ cup chopped cilantro before pureeing. For a hotter salsa, do not seed the jalapeños.

Arroz con Pollo

Each of the Spanish-speaking countries of the world has its favorite way of making this casserole. Sometimes it is flavored with achiote seeds, sometimes with saffron, and sometimes with both. You have all those options here. I have used skinless and boneless chicken thighs because the meat stays moist and it is very easy to serve and eat. This casserole tastes best one to three hours after cooking.

Makes: 6 to 8 servings

Bakes: At 325° F. for about 30 minutes

Casserole: Choose a 4-quart flameproof casserole (such as an enameled cast-iron dutch oven)

3 tablespoons achiote oil (see Note) or vegetable oil

1½ pounds skinless and boneless chicken thighs (3 pounds before skinning and boning)

3 tablespoons cider vinegar or wine vinegar

2 teaspoons dried oregano, crumbled

2 onions, coarsely chopped

2 green bell peppers, cored and coarsely chopped

2½ cups long-grain white rice

2 large garlic cloves, minced or crushed through a press

4 ounces smoked ham, cut into ¼ × 2-inch sticks (1 cup)

1 can (14 to 16 ounces) whole tomatoes, drained, seeded, coarsely chopped, and drained again

3 cups chicken stock or canned broth

½ cup dry sherry, white wine, or beer

2 bay leaves

¼ teaspoon saffron threads (optional)

½ teaspoon salt

¼ teaspoon black pepper

2 large red bell peppers, roasted, peeled, and cut into ½ × 2-inch strips

½ cup sliced pimiento-stuffed green olives

¼ cup chopped fresh parsley (optional)

1 tablespoon capers (optional)

1 package (10 ounces) frozen peas, thawed slightly

1. Prepare the achiote oil and let it cool while you continue.

2. Cut the chicken across the grain into ½-inch-wide strips about 2 inches long. Place in a large bowl and toss with the vinegar and oregano. Let marinate at room temperature for 1 hour, or cover and refrigerate for as long as 6 hours.

3. Drain the chicken in a sieve over a bowl, reserving the marinade. Place the casserole over high heat. Spoon in 1½ tablespoons of the achiote oil. Arrange half of the chicken in the hot oil and let brown very well, without stirring, about 5 minutes. Turn the pieces with tongs and brown for 1 to 2 minutes longer. Take out and reserve. Spoon in ½ tablespoon more oil and brown the remaining chicken.

4. Pour the remaining 1 tablespoon achiote oil into the casserole and set over moderate heat. Add the onions and green bell peppers and sauté until softened, about 5 minutes.

5. Add the rice and sauté, stirring frequently, until lightly browned, 3 to 5 minutes. Add the garlic and ham and cook for 2 minutes longer. Add the tomatoes, any reserved marinade, chicken stock, sherry, bay leaves, saffron, salt, and pepper. Bring quickly to a boil over high heat. Lower the heat and simmer, uncovered, stirring occasionally, until no longer soupy, about 15 minutes.

6. Meanwhile, adjust an oven shelf to the lower third of the oven and preheat the oven.

7. When the rice has cooked for about 15 minutes, remove the casserole from the heat and stir in the chicken, roasted red bell peppers, olives, parsley, and capers. Bake, uncovered, for 15 minutes.

8. Scatter the peas over the top of the casserole. Cover and bake for about 15 minutes, or until the rice is tender and the peas are heated through. Uncover and let stand for at least 10 minutes before serving. Toss gently and serve hot.

Variations: Use 4 pounds of whole chicken parts in place of the sliced thighs, although the browned breast pieces should not be added until after the initial 15-minute simmer with the rice; add them before baking and cook until no longer pink at the bone. One cup of store-bought pimiento strips can be used in place of the roasted red peppers. Additional chicken stock can be used in place of the sherry, wine, or beer.

Reheat: This casserole tastes best on the day it is made. It will stay warm in the pan for several hours. If at room temperature, cover and bake at 325° F. for about 30 minutes.

Note: To make achiote oil: Combine 3½ tablespoons vegetable oil with 2 to 3 tablespoons whole achiote (annatto) seeds in a small skillet or saucepan. Place over low heat and sizzle gently until the oil turns bright orange, 2 to 3 minutes. Remove from the heat and let cool. Strain out and discard the solids.

Turkey Ranchero Casserole

This is simpler and lighter than most other Southwestern casseroles because you layer the corn tortillas without frying them first. It's a casserole that you can really sink your teeth into.

MAKES: 8 servings

BAKES: At 350° F. for 50 to 60 minutes

CASSEROLE: Lightly oil a 13 × 9 × 2-inch casserole

1 pound boiling or all-purpose potatoes (3 to 4 medium)

4 slices lean smoked bacon, chopped

2 onions, chopped

1 large garlic clove, minced

½ teaspoon dried oregano, crumbled

½ teaspoon ground cumin

2 teaspoons salt

¼ teaspoon black pepper

1½ pounds ground turkey (half thigh, half breast if grinding at home)

2 tablespoons all-purpose flour

2 cans (8 ounces each) tomato sauce

½ cup water

12 corn tortillas (12 to 14 ounces), quartered

2 cups homemade (see page 20) or store-bought medium-hot salsa

1½ cups Monterey Jack cheese, grated (6 ounces)

1½ cups sharp cheddar cheese, grated (6 ounces)

1½ cups sour cream (low-fat is okay), at room temperature

24 mild black olives

1. Bring a large pot of lightly salted water to a boil over high heat. Meanwhile, peel the potatoes and cut them into ½-inch dice. Drop the potatoes into the boiling water and cook until tender, about 5 minutes. Drain and reserve.

2. Preheat the oven, and prepare the casserole.

3. Place a nonreactive large skillet over moderate heat. Add the bacon and cook until crisp and golden brown. Tilt the pan and spoon off all but 1 tablespoon of the fat. Return the pan to the heat and add the onions; sauté to soften, adding 1 to 2 tablespoons water if dry, about 5 minutes.

4. Add the garlic, oregano, cumin, salt, and pepper to the skillet and cook for 1 minute longer. Push the mixture to one side of the pan and crumble in the ground turkey. Increase the heat to moderately high and lightly brown the meat, stirring occasionally, for 3 to 4 minutes. Sprinkle the flour over the top and stir to moisten. Add 1 can of the tomato sauce and the water. Cook until thickened, 2 to 3 minutes. Add the potatoes and toss to combine.

5. Spread half of the remaining can of tomato sauce in the prepared casserole. Arrange 6 of the tortillas over the bottom in an overlapping layer. Spoon on half of the salsa, and then half of the turkey filling. Combine the 2 cheeses and toss; sprinkle half of the cheese over the turkey. Repeat the layering; spoon the remaining canned tomato sauce over the cheese.

6. Bake for 50 to 60 minutes, or until hot and golden brown. Cut into 8 squares and serve hot; top each portion with 3 tablespoons of the sour cream and 3 of the black olives.

Variations: Half of the cheese can be eliminated to lighten this casserole. Ground beef, chicken, or pork can replace the ground turkey. Cilantro and sliced scallions can be used as garnishes, if desired.

Reheat: Pour ½ cup water over the top and cover with aluminum foil. If at room temperature, bake at 350° F. for 35 minutes. Uncover and bake for about 10 minutes longer, or until hot; if cold, add about 15 minutes before uncovering.

Turkey and Stuffing Casserole

This is a totally different concept of a turkey and stuffing casserole from the one that precedes it. Here, you start with raw ground turkey instead of a roasted turkey and you line the casserole with it to make a "shell" that's filled with stuffing—all the flavors of turkey and stuffing but none of the fuss.

MAKES: 8 servings
BAKES: At 325° F. for 1½ hours
CASSEROLE: Oil a deep 3-quart casserole

Turkey shell

1 tablespoon olive oil, butter, or vegetable oil

1 onion, chopped

1 large garlic clove, minced

½ teaspoon ground or rubbed sage

1½ pounds ground turkey

8 ounces fresh mushrooms, grated on the coarse side of a cheese grater or ground in a food processor

2 large eggs

½ cup plain dry bread crumbs

¼ cup dry white wine

1 tablespoon sweet paprika

¾ teaspoon salt

Stuffing

1 tablespoon olive oil

1 tablespoon unsalted butter

1½ cups finely chopped celery

2 onions, chopped

1 large garlic clove, minced

½ teaspoon ground or rubbed sage

½ pound ground turkey

2 large eggs

⅓ cup dry white wine

1 bag (8 ounces) plain stuffing mix (4 cups crumbs or croutons)

½ cup chopped fresh parsley

⅓ cup chopped celery leaves (optional)

¾ teaspoon salt

¾ cup chicken broth

1. **Turkey shell:** Preheat the oven, and prepare the casserole.

2. In a medium skillet, combine the olive oil and onion over moderate heat. Sauté to soften and lightly brown, adding 1 to 2 tablespoons water if dry, 4 to

5 minutes. Add the garlic and sage and cook for 1 minute longer. Remove from the heat.

3. Crumble the ground turkey into a large bowl. Add the grated mushrooms, eggs, bread crumbs, wine, paprika, and salt. Scrape the onion mixture over the top. Mix with your hands to blend well.

4. Stuffing: Combine the olive oil and butter in a large skillet over moderate heat. Add the celery and onions, and sauté to soften, 4 to 5 minutes. Stir in the garlic and sage and cook for about 30 seconds longer. Remove from the heat.

5. Crumble the ground turkey into a large bowl. Add the eggs and wine, and blend vigorously with your hands or a large spoon to combine ingredients. Add the stuffing mix, parsley, celery leaves, and salt. Toss to combine the ingredients. Gradually add the broth and toss to moisten.

6. Assembly: Remove and reserve 1½ cups of the turkey shell mixture for the top and turn the rest into the casserole. Pat the mixture over the bottom and three-fourths of the way up the sides of the casserole to make an even shell about ¾ inch thick. Loosely pack the stuffing in the center. Top with the reserved turkey shell mixture, and use wet fingers to pat it into an even layer over the stuffing. Pinch the edges all around to seal. Poke a 1-inch hole in the center with your finger or the back of a spoon.

7. Cover the casserole and bake for about 1½ hours, or until the internal temperature is about 165° F. (it will rise about 10° after removing from the oven). Let stand for about 15 minutes before serving. Cut into wedges so each portion is a cross-section.

Variations: Ground chicken, pork, veal, or beef, or a combination of any or all, can be used in place of the turkey. Toasted crumbled corn bread can be used in place of croutons.

Reheat: Add ¼ cup water and cover casserole. If at room temperature, bake at 350° F. for 30 to 40 minutes; if cold, add 15 minutes.

| Turkey Dinner in a Pot |

Here is a great use for Thanksgiving leftovers–a casserole of stuffing, sliced turkey, mashed potatoes, and gravy. Although I have given instructions here for making the stuffing, you can skip step 2 if you have about 4 cups leftover stuffing. I recommend serving two vegetables–such as corn and green beans–alongside this casserole, and don't skip the cranberry sauce.

MAKES: 8 servings

BAKES: At 375° F. for about 35 minutes

CASSEROLE: Lightly oil a 13 × 9 × 2-inch casserole

2 tablespoons butter

1 cup finely chopped celery

1 onion, chopped

½ teaspoon ground or rubbed dried sage

1 bag (8 ounces) plain stuffing mix (or 4 cups crumbs or croutons)

¾ to 1 cup chicken or turkey stock or canned broth

¼ cup dry white wine

¼ to ½ cup chopped celery leaves (from the heart; optional)

¼ cup chopped fresh parsley (optional)

2 cups turkey gravy

About 1 pound sliced cooked turkey breast and thigh meat

4 cups mashed potatoes

2 tablespoons freshly grated Parmesan cheese

Cranberry sauce, for serving (optional)

1. Adjust an oven shelf to the top third of the oven and preheat the oven. Prepare the casserole.

2. Melt the butter in a medium skillet over moderate heat. Add the celery and onion, and cook until softened, 3 to 5 minutes. Stir in the sage and cook 1 minute longer. Turn into a large bowl and add the stuffing mix; toss to combine. Pour ¾ cup of the broth all over and toss. Add the wine, celery leaves, and parsley; toss. For a moister stuffing, add the remaining ¼ cup broth.

3. Spread ½ cup of the gravy in the casserole. Add the stuffing and pat into an even layer. Arrange the turkey slices all over, almost covering the stuffing.

Spread another ½ cup of the gravy over the turkey. Spoon the mashed pota-toes into eight ½-cup mounds over the top; make an indentation with the back of a spoon to form a well in each mound. Spoon the remaining 1 cup gravy into the mounds, letting any excess run over. Sprinkle on the Parmesan.

4. Bake in the top third of the oven until browned and bubbly, about 35 min-utes. Serve hot, with cranberry sauce.

Variations: Use chicken or sliced pork loin instead of turkey. If you have a favorite stuffing recipe, follow it and use 4 cups in place of this one. You can also add ¼ cup chopped parsley to the mashed potatoes.

Reheat: Spoon ¼ cup of water around the edges and down the center of the casserole. Cover with foil and bake at 350° F. for 25 to 30 minutes; if cold, add about 15 minutes.

Scalloped Oysters

Cod in Dill Cream with Duchesse Potatoes

Codfish Casserole with Tomato Sauce

Creamy Salmon and Linguine Casserole

Shrimps and Rice

Tuna-Noodle Casserole

Fresh Tuna-Noodle Casserole

| Seafood |

Tuna Bro Casserole

Tuna and Potato Casserole with Leeks

Tuna and Olive Parmesan Batter Bake

Salmon-Potato Casserole with Broccoli

Salmon-Asparagus Casserole
with Parsleyed Rice

Brown Rice Paella

Scalloped Oysters

I have boosted the flavor of this old-fashioned American favorite with bacon, lemon, and just a dab of anchovy paste for depth. Since the oysters are baked, it's okay to buy cartons of shucked oysters.

MAKES: 4 to 6 servings
BAKES: At 375° F. for 35 to 40 minutes
CASSEROLE: Butter a shallow 1½- to 2-quart casserole

3 cups shucked oysters, with liquor

4 slices lean smoked bacon, chopped

1½ cups coarse cracker crumbs, from saltines or oyster crackers

2 tablespoons butter, cut into bits

2 tablespoons fresh lemon juice

1 teaspoon anchovy paste

1 cup heavy cream

¼ cup dry sherry or white wine

½ teaspoon salt

⅛ teaspoon black pepper

½ teaspoon sweet paprika

2 tablespoons chopped fresh parsley

1. Adjust an oven shelf to the top third of the oven. Preheat the oven, and prepare the casserole.

2. Drain the oysters and reserve ½ cup of the liquor (juice). If you should happen to have less, add water, clam juice, or wine to make up the difference.

3. Cook the bacon in a heavy, medium skillet over moderate heat until crisp and golden brown. Drain on paper towels.

4. Sprinkle ½ cup of the cracker crumbs into the casserole and arrange half of the oysters on top. Sprinkle on the bacon and dot with 1 tablespoon of the butter. Repeat with ½ cup more cracker crumbs, the remaining oysters, and the remaining 1 tablespoon butter.

5. In a medium bowl, combine the lemon juice and anchovy paste; stir with a fork to blend. Stir in the cream, sherry, salt, pepper, and the reserved ½ cup oyster liquor. Pour over the oysters. Sprinkle the remaining ½ cup crumbs and the paprika over the top.

6. Bake, uncovered, in the top third of the oven for 35 to 40 minutes, or until vigorously bubbly and speckled brown on top. Let stand for 5 minutes before serving. Sprinkle with the parsley and serve hot.

Variations: Omit the bacon and add 2 tablespoons chopped parsley after the first layer of oysters. Replace the heavy cream with light cream, half-and-half, or whole milk, but do not stir the lemon juice into the mixture; instead, splash the lemon juice over the first layer of oysters.

Reheat: If at room temperature, heat in the top third of a 375° F. oven for about 30 minutes; if cold, add 10 to 15 minutes.

Cod in Dill Cream with Duchesse Potatoes

This beautiful and elegant casserole of Irish inspiration is good for entertaining. I do recommend piping the mashed potatoes through a wide star tip, but you also have the option of spooning the mixture around the chunks of cod.

MAKES: 6 servings
BAKES: At 400° F. for 20 to 25 minutes
CASSEROLE: Butter a 13 × 9 × 2-inch casserole or oval gratin dish

6 thick pieces (6 ounces each) skinless and boneless cod

3 tablespoons unsalted butter

1 onion, minced

1 cup light cream or milk

1 cup milk

3 tablespoons snipped fresh dill

2 bay leaves

¼ cup all-purpose flour

¼ cup dry white wine

1 teaspoon salt

1 recipe Duchesse Potatoes (recipe follows)

1. Feel the codfish with your fingers and pull out any bones with pliers.

2. Position an oven shelf in the top third of the oven and preheat the oven. Prepare the casserole.

3. Choose a wide skillet or sauté pan large enough to hold the fish in a single layer. Add 1 tablespoon of the butter to the pan and place over low heat. Add the onion and sauté gently to soften but not color, 3 to 5 minutes. Pour in the cream and milk, and add 2 tablespoons of the dill and the bay leaves.

4. Arrange the cod in the pan and spoon some of the cream over them. Bring to a simmer over moderate heat. Reduce the heat to low, cover, and poach until almost cooked through, 5 to 7 minutes (they will bake and cook further later). Uncover and spoon some of the cream over the cod once or twice during the poaching time. Uncover and remove the pan from the heat.

5. With a slotted spatula, carefully remove the cod and evenly space the pieces in the prepared casserole; remember, the potato will be piped around and between the pieces. If any of the poaching cream accumulates, spoon it back into the skillet.

6. Melt the remaining 2 tablespoons butter in a small skillet over moderate heat. Add the flour and stir for about 2 minutes to cook the flour. Place the skillet of poaching cream over moderate heat and bring to a boil. Add the flour mixture and whisk until thick and simmering. Add the wine, salt, and the remaining 1 tablespoon dill. Cook, stirring occasionally, 2 to 3 minutes longer. Spoon all of the cream sauce over the cod. This can be assembled an hour ahead and kept covered with waxed paper.

7. Fit a pastry bag with a ¾-inch star tip and fill with the Duchesse Potatoes. Pipe a wide shell border down the center of the casserole, between the cod pieces, and crosswise twice to separate the pieces. Pipe a wide shell border all around the edge. Pipe a rosette in the center of each piece of cod.

8. Bake for 20 to 25 minutes, or until the potatoes are golden brown and the sauce is bubbly. Let stand for 5 minutes. Serve hot.

Variations: Use scrod, haddock, or salmon in place of the cod. Basil can be used instead of dill. Or, eliminate the dill and use 4 bay leaves instead. If desired, arrange in 6 individual casseroles and pipe potatoes around each as above.

Reheat: This casserole tastes best freshly baked, although you can keep it hot in the turned-off oven for 30 to 60 minutes.

| Duchesse Potatoes |

These are simply rich French mashed potatoes fortified with egg. Use them to pipe over casseroles for an elegant, decorative effect.

MAKES: About 6 cups

**3 pounds russet baking potatoes
(6 large)**

½ cup light cream

2 tablespoons unsalted butter

1 teaspoon salt

**¼ teaspoon freshly grated
nutmeg**

1 large egg

2 large egg yolks

1. Peel the potatoes and cut them into 1-inch chunks, dropping them into a large pot of cold water as they are cut.

2. Partially cover the pot and bring to a boil over moderately high heat. Boil until the potatoes are tender when pierced with a fork, 15 to 20 minutes. Drain in a colander and return to the pot. Shake over moderate heat for about 30 seconds to dry.

3. Add the cream, butter, salt, and nutmeg; beat with a hand-held electric mixer until fluffy. Let cool for about 10 minutes, or keep warm in a pan placed over hot water until ready to assemble the casserole.

4. Beat in the egg and egg yolks. Fill a pastry bag fitted with a large star tip. Pipe the potatoes over the casserole. Brown in the top third of a 400° F. oven for 20 to 25 minutes.

Codfish Casserole with Tomato Sauce

Although this is delicious all by itself, the recipe makes abundant sauce as it bakes, so consider serving it over rice, linguine, or sliced boiled potatoes.

MAKES: 4 servings

BAKES: At 425° F. for 20 to 25 minutes

CASSEROLE: Generously coat a shallow 12 × 8-inch casserole or gratin dish with olive oil

2 tablespoons olive oil

2 onions, chopped

2 green bell peppers, trimmed and cut into ½-inch squares

4 tablespoons chopped fresh parsley

2 large garlic cloves, minced

½ teaspoon dried thyme, crumbled

1 can (28 ounces) whole tomatoes, drained, seeded, and coarsely chopped

½ cup dry white wine

1 teaspoon salt

1½ pounds scrod or codfish fillets (1 inch thick)

1. Adjust an oven shelf to the top third of the oven. Preheat the oven, and prepare the casserole.

2. Spoon the olive oil into a nonreactive large skillet and place over moderate heat. Add the onions and bell peppers, and sauté to soften, about 5 minutes. Add 1 to 2 tablespoons water if the mixture seems dry. Add 2 tablespoons of the parsley, along with the garlic and thyme; cook for 1 to 2 minutes longer. Add the tomatoes, reserving the juice for another use. Add the wine and ¾ teaspoon of the salt; bring to a boil over moderately high heat. Boil until thick and reduced to 2½ to 3 cups, about 10 minutes.

3. Meanwhile, cut the fish into 1½-inch squares. Arrange the squares in the prepared casserole. Sprinkle with the remaining ¼ teaspoon salt.

4. Spoon all of the tomato sauce over the fish. Bake until the fish is cooked through and flakes easily, 20 to 25 minutes. Sprinkle with the remaining 2 tablespoons parsley and serve hot.

Variations: To add a little zing, stir ½ teaspoon of dried red pepper flakes into the sauce. Fresh basil or cilantro can replace the parsley. For a Spanish note, ¼ cup sliced green olives and 1 tablespoon capers can be added.

Reheat: If at room temperature, cover and bake at 350° F. for 20 to 30 minutes; if cold, add about 15 minutes.

Creamy Salmon and Linguine Casserole

Large flakes of pink salmon make this look as good as it tastes. Broccoli, green beans, or asparagus taste great alongside.

MAKES: 6 to 8 servings
BAKES: At 425° F. for 25 to 30 minutes
CASSEROLE: Butter or oil a 13 × 9 × 2-inch casserole

1 bottle (8 ounces) clam juice
½ cup dry white wine
¼ cup water
2 bay leaves
5 whole cloves
2 large garlic cloves, 1 sliced and 1 minced
2 pounds salmon steaks, cut 1 inch thick
3 tablespoons olive oil
3 tablespoons unsalted butter
1 cup chopped shallots or onion

¼ to ½ teaspoon dried red pepper flakes
¼ cup plus 2 tablespoons all-purpose flour
2 cups chicken stock or canned broth
½ cup heavy cream
1½ teaspoons salt
¼ cup chopped fresh dill
2 tablespoons fresh lemon juice
1 pound linguine, broken in half
¼ cup chopped fresh parsley

1. Choose a nonreactive sauté pan or wide saucepan just large enough to hold the salmon steaks in a single layer. In the pan, combine the clam juice, wine, water, bay leaves, cloves, and sliced garlic. Simmer over low heat for 5 minutes.

2. Add the salmon steaks to the pan, cover, and poach gently for 5 minutes. Carefully turn and poach for about 7 minutes longer, until just cooked through.

3. With a slotted spatula, transfer the fish to a platter to cool. Strain the poaching broth. If fatty, degrease by blotting quickly with a paper towel. You will need 1½ cups of poaching broth; if necessary, add water. Remove the skin and bones from the salmon and break the meat into large flakes.

4. Adjust an oven shelf to the top third. Preheat the oven, and prepare the casserole. Bring a large pot of lightly salted water to a boil.

5. Meanwhile, in a large saucepan, combine the olive oil and butter over moderate heat. Add the shallots, minced garlic, and pepper flakes; sauté to soften, 3 to 5 minutes. Stir in the flour and cook for 1 to 2 minutes; the mixture will be dry. Stir in the reserved 1½ cups poaching broth and the chicken stock; stir until smooth and simmering. Add the cream and simmer, stirring occasionally, until thickened, 3 to 4 minutes. Turn the sauce into a large bowl; fold in the salmon, salt, dill, and lemon juice.

6. Drop the linguine into the boiling water and stir until the boil resumes, and then frequently thereafter. Boil until tender but firm to the bite, 10 to 12 minutes. Drain in a colander and shake out any excess water.

7. Add the pasta to the salmon and sauce and toss. Turn into the prepared casserole. Bake in the top third of the oven for 25 to 30 minutes, or until the top is well browned and the edges are bubbly. Serve hot, sprinkled with the parsley.

Variations: You can substitute three 15-ounce cans of pink salmon for the fresh; simply drain and use 1 cup of the juices to replace the clam juice. Remove the skin and bones from the salmon and the yield will be about 1½ pounds, the same yield as 2 pounds of fresh salmon after cooking, skinning, and boning. One teaspoon dried dill can be used in place of fresh dill. For a flavor change, use fresh basil instead of dill. Sliced sautéed mushrooms can be added along with the salmon.

Reheat: Pour ½ cup water over the casserole; cover with foil. If at room temperature, reheat in the top third of a 350° F. oven for about 20 minutes. Uncover, increase the heat to 425° F., and bake for about 10 minutes longer to crisp the top. If the casserole was cold, add 10 to 15 minutes before increasing the oven temperature.

| Shrimps and Rice |

As that old song goes, "Shrimps and rice . . . are very nice." This
elegant recipe came to me from my favorite Auntie Myra's girlfriend, Astrid
Sinkler. They've been best friends since the fourth grade during the 1920s in
Ashtabula Harbor, Ohio. Myra always raves about this pretty casserole, with
the pink shrimps showing through the golden buttered-crumb topping. So I
asked Astrid for the recipe, and I am proud to include it here.

MAKES: 8 servings
BAKES: At 350° F. for about 45 minutes
CASSEROLE: Butter a 13 × 9 × 2-inch casserole

1½ **pounds small to medium
    shrimp**

1½ **cups long-grain white rice**

4 **tablespoons unsalted butter**

1½ **cups finely diced celery**

1 **green bell pepper, finely
   chopped**

1 **onion, finely chopped**

8 **ounces fresh mushrooms,
   thinly sliced**

½ **cup finely chopped pimiento**

1 **teaspoon grated lemon zest**

3 **tablespoons fresh lemon juice**

2 **teaspoons salt**

½ **teaspoon black pepper**

1 **pint low-fat sour cream**

1 **cup half-and-half**

1¼ **cups fresh soft bread
    crumbs, made from firm
    homemade-style white bread**

2 **tablespoons minced fresh
   parsley**

1. Bring a large pot of water to a boil over high heat. Meanwhile, peel the
shrimp and devein if desired; set aside.

2. Gradually add the rice to the boiling water. Stir occasionally and boil until
firm-tender, about 12 minutes. Drain in a sieve, shaking until the dripping
stops. Turn the rice into a large bowl.

3. Preheat the oven, and prepare the casserole.

4. Melt 2 tablespoons of the butter in a large skillet over moderate heat. Add the celery, bell pepper, and onion, and sauté to soften, about 5 minutes. Add the mushrooms, increase the heat to high, and sauté to soften, 2 to 3 minutes. Turn the mixture out over the rice. Add the pimiento, lemon zest, lemon juice, 1½ teaspoons of the salt, and all of the pepper; toss to combine the ingredients.

5. In a medium bowl, stir together the sour cream, half-and-half, and the remaining ½ teaspoon salt. Remove 1 cup of this mixture and stir it into the rice mixture.

6. Turn the rice mixture into the prepared casserole and spread in an even layer. Arrange all of the shrimp over the rice and spread the remaining sour cream mixture over the top.

7. Melt the remaining 2 tablespoons butter in a medium skillet over moderate heat. Add the bread crumbs and toss to coat. Sprinkle evenly over the casserole. Bake for about 45 minutes, or until golden brown. Serve hot, sprinkled with the parsley.

Variations: Use a combination of ½ pound each shrimp, scallops, and crabmeat. Regular sour cream can be used instead of low-fat. Two tablespoons snipped fresh dill can be added when tossing the rice with the other ingredients.

Reheat: Cover the casserole tightly with aluminum foil. If at room temperature, bake in top third of a 350° F. oven for about 25 minutes. Uncover, increase the oven temperature to 450° F., and bake until the crumbs are crispy, about 10 minutes longer; if cold, add about 15 minutes before increasing the oven temperature.

Tuna-Noodle Casserole

I lost more than a few night's sleep over this recipe. In general, I don't cook with canned soups and convenience foods, so it seemed that I should make this from fresh tuna steaks and a homemade cream sauce. But everyone I questioned on the subject said no, that I should make it with canned cream of mushroom soup, just like their mothers did. But I couldn't help adding a little wine to freshen up the canned ingredients. And don't pass up the fresh version (recipe follows).

MAKES: 4 servings
BAKES: At 425° F. for 25 to 30 minutes
CASSEROLE: Lightly oil an 8- or 9-inch shallow casserole

1 tablespoon unsalted butter or olive oil

8 ounces fresh mushrooms, thinly sliced

1 teaspoon dried oregano, crumbled

2 cans (10¾ ounces each) condensed cream of mushroom soup

¼ cup milk

¼ cup dry white wine

2 cans (6 to 6½ ounces each) water-packed chunk light tuna, undrained

½ teaspoon salt

¼ teaspoon black pepper

8 ounces wide egg noodles

½ cup finely crushed potato chips, or 3 tablespoons plain dry bread crumbs

1. Preheat the oven, and prepare the casserole. Bring a large pot of lightly salted water to a boil over high heat.

2. Meanwhile, melt the butter in a large skillet over moderate heat. Add the mushrooms and oregano, increase the heat to high, and brown for 1 to 2 minutes. Toss, add 1 tablespoon water, and cook for 1 minute longer, until tender. Reserve.

3. In a large bowl, stir together the undiluted soup with the milk. Stir in the wine and the undrained tuna, breaking up the large pieces with a fork. Stir in the sautéed mushrooms, salt, and pepper.

4. Drop the noodles into the boiling water and stir until the boil resumes. Cook, stirring frequently, until tender, 8 to 10 minutes. Drain in a colander and add to the tuna mixture.

5. Turn the mixture into the prepared casserole. Sprinkle the crushed potato chips on top. Bake 25 to 30 minutes, or until deep golden brown on top and bubbly around the edges. Let stand for at least 10 minutes before serving.

Variations: You can use tuna packed in oil for this, but be sure to drain it thoroughly and add an extra tablespoon each of milk and wine. You can also use canned mushrooms for the fresh and eliminate the butter.

Reheat: This casserole tastes best fresh. If you must reheat it, sprinkle with 2 to 3 tablespoons of water. If at room temperature, bake at 350° F. for about 25 minutes; if cold, add 10 to 15 minutes.

Fresh Tuna-Noodle Casserole

I cook with more fresh ingredients than canned so I couldn't resist creating a fresh version of this classic casserole.

MAKES: 4 servings

BAKES: At 425° F. for 18 to 20 minutes

CASSEROLE: Lightly oil an 8- or 9-inch shallow casserole

1 pound fresh skinless and boneless tuna steaks

2 tablespoons fresh lemon juice

4 tablespoons unsalted butter

8 ounces fresh mushrooms, sliced

⅓ cup all-purpose flour

2 cups low-fat or whole milk

2 tablespoons cornstarch

1 bottle (8 ounces) clam juice, or 1 cup fish stock

¼ cup dry white wine

1 teaspoon salt

¼ teaspoon freshly grated nutmeg

¼ teaspoon black pepper

8 ounces wide egg noodles

2 tablespoons snipped fresh dill, or 1 teaspoon dried oregano, crumbled

½ cup crushed potato chips, or 3 tablespoons bread crumbs

1. Cut the tuna steaks into sticks about ½ inch thick and 1½ to 2 inches long. Combine in a nonreactive dish with the fresh lemon juice and marinate in the refrigerator while you continue.

2. Preheat the oven, and prepare the casserole. Bring a large saucepan of salted water to a boil.

3. Meanwhile, melt 1 tablespoon of the butter in a large skillet over moderate heat. Add the mushrooms and brown, without stirring, for 1 to 2 minutes. Stir and add about 1 tablespoon water; cook about 1 minute longer, until tender.

4. Melt the remaining 3 tablespoons butter in a medium saucepan over moderate heat. Stir in the flour and cook, stirring, for a minute or two. The mixture will be dry. Pour in the milk; bring to a simmer, stirring constantly.

5. In a bowl, stir together the cornstarch, clam juice, and wine. Pour into the sauce, stirring. Add the salt, nutmeg, and pepper. Simmer for 2 to 3 minutes to thicken.

6. Drop the noodles into boiling water. Stir until the boil returns; boil under tender, 8 to 10 minutes. Drain.

7. Combine the noodles with the sauce, tuna, and mushrooms. Add the dill or oregano and turn into the prepared casserole; top with the potato chips or bread crumbs.

8. Bake in the top third of the oven for 18 to 20 minutes, or until golden brown and bubbly. Let stand for 10 minutes before serving.

Variations: Use swordfish, monkfish, or mako shark in place of tuna. Add ¼ cup chopped roasted red pepper or pimiento.

Reheat: If at room temperature, bake at 350° F. for about 20 minutes; if cold, add 10 to 15 minutes.

| Tuna Bro Casserole |

It's good to have a few special recipes that call for canned tuna. This one is a casserole layered with potatoes, broccoli, and cheese sauce and flavored with celery seeds. It's super for supper or lunch and can be made a day in advance.

MAKES: 4 to 6 servings
BAKES: At 400° F. for 35 to 40 minutes
CASSEROLE: Oil or butter a shallow 2-quart casserole

4 cups lightly packed broccoli florets (about 12 ounces)

1½ pounds (5 to 6 medium) red-skinned potatoes, peeled and cut into ¼-inch slices

3 tablespoons unsalted butter

¼ cup plus 2 tablespoons all-purpose flour

3 cups milk

1 teaspoon salt

½ teaspoon celery seeds

1½ cups grated sharp cheddar cheese (6 ounces)

1 can (6 to 7 ounces) water-packed solid white tuna, drained

1 can (6 to 7 ounces) water-packed chunk light tuna, drained

½ teaspoon sweet paprika

1. Bring a large pot of lightly salted water to a boil over high heat. Drop in the broccoli, partially cover, and bring back to a boil. Boil for 2 minutes; scoop out with a slotted spoon and drain. Add the potatoes to the water, partially cover, and return to a boil. Cook for 2 minutes; drain.

2. Preheat the oven, and prepare the casserole.

3. Melt the butter in a medium saucepan over moderate heat. Stir in the flour and cook for 2 minutes; the mixture will be dry. Pour in 1 cup of the milk and stir until smooth. Add the remaining 2 cups milk, along with the salt and celery seeds; stir until thick and simmering. Cook, stirring frequently, for 2 to 3 minutes longer. Remove from the heat and stir in the cheese until melted and smooth.

4. Spread ¼ cup of the cheese sauce in the casserole. Add the potatoes in an even layer. Spoon on ¾ cup more sauce. Break both the white and light tuna into large flakes and scatter on top of the sauce. Cover with the broccoli, pressing to make an even layer. Pour on the remaining sauce; sprinkle with the paprika.

5. Bake in the center of the oven for 35 to 40 minutes, or until browned and bubbly. Let stand for at least 15 minutes before serving.

Variations: The tuna can be oil-packed if desired and you can use all white or light tuna as desired. Omit the celery seeds and replace with ¼ teaspoon freshly grated nutmeg. To cut some fat and calories, reduce the cheese to 4 ounces. One-quarter cup white wine can replace part of the milk, but add it last, after the sauce has thickened. Also, ⅛ teaspoon cayenne pepper can be added for a spark of flavor.

Reheat: If at room temperature, bake at 350° F. for 30 to 35 minutes; if cold, cover with foil and reheat at 350° F. for 30 minutes. Then, uncover and heat for about 20 minutes longer.

Tuna and Potato Casserole with Leeks

Easy, economical, hearty, and relatively low in fat, this casserole should please all tuna and potato lovers. It's also a good showcase for leeks.

MAKES: 4 to 6 servings
BAKES: At 350° F. for about 45 minutes
CASSEROLE: Oil a shallow 2-quart casserole

2 pounds russet baking potatoes (6 medium)

3 or 4 leeks

1 tablespoon olive oil

2 large eggs

3 tablespoons all-purpose flour

1 cup light or regular sour cream

1 cut low-fat plain yogurt

1 tablespoon fresh lemon juice

1½ teaspoons salt

½ teaspoon ground cumin

¼ teaspoon black pepper

1 can (6 to 7 ounces) water-packed solid white tuna, undrained

1 can (6 to 7 ounces) water-packed chunk light tuna, undrained

¼ cup freshly grated Parmesan cheese (1 ounce)

½ teaspoon sweet paprika

1. Place the potatoes in a large pot and add cold water to cover generously. Place over moderately high heat, partially cover, and boil until tender when pierced with a fork, 40 to 45 minutes. Drain and set aside until cool enough to handle.

2. Cut off the roots from the leeks. Also, cut off the darkest green portions of the leaves and any soft or wilted outer layers of leaves, leaving just the white, light-, and medium-green portions. Cut lengthwise in half and then crosswise into ½-inch pieces. Rinse well in a large bowl of cool water to dislodge any sand. Scoop out the pieces (they float) and transfer to a strainer to drain, leaving any sand or grit behind in the bowl. Roll up in paper towels to dry. There should be about 3 cups.

3. Preheat the oven, and prepare the casserole.

4. Spoon the olive oil into a heavy, medium skillet and place over moderate heat. Add the leeks and sauté to soften and lightly brown, adding 1 to 2 tablespoons water if dry, about 5 minutes.

5. In a large bowl, whisk the eggs with the flour. Whisk in the sour cream, yogurt, lemon juice, salt, cumin, and pepper.

6. Peel 2 of the potatoes and mash them. Add to the sour cream mixture. Cut the remaining unpeeled potatoes into 1-inch chunks and add them along with the sautéed leeks. Add both cans of tuna, with the water, and separate into large flakes. Toss to combine the ingredients.

7. Turn the mixture into the prepared casserole; sprinkle the Parmesan and paprika over the top. Bake for about 45 minutes, or until browned on top and bubbly around the edges. Let cool for at least 10 minutes before serving.

Variations: Although the flavor will be different (but still delicious), substitute 2 medium onions, chopped, for the leeks, and add 1 large minced garlic clove, if desired. Sliced or whole pitted black olives can be added, and so can ¼ cup chopped fresh parsley.

Reheat: If at room temperature, reheat at 350° F. for about 35 minutes; if cold, reheat for about 1 hour.

Tuna and Olive Parmesan Batter Bake

Brown rice and peas, enriched with cream cheese, make the base for a moist mixture of tuna and black olives with sour cream. A quick yeast batter is fortified with Parmesan cheese and dotted with sesame seeds to encase the layers.

MAKES: 8 servings

BAKES: At 350° F. for 45 to 50 minutes

CASSEROLE: Butter or oil a 13 × 9 × 2-inch casserole

1 pound fresh mushrooms, sliced

1 cup long-grain brown rice

1 package (10 ounces) frozen peas, thawed slightly

½ large package (4 ounces) cream cheese, at room temperature

3 large eggs

1 cup freshly grated Parmesan cheese (4 ounces)

1 teaspoon salt

¼ teaspoon black pepper

1¾ cups sour cream, at room temperature

1½ cups all-purpose flour

½ teaspoon dried dill, or 1 tablespoon chopped fresh dill

2 cans (6 to 7 ounces each) water-packed solid white tuna, drained and broken into large flakes

2 hard-cooked large eggs, chopped

1 can (7 ounces) pitted black olives, drained

3 tablespoons melted unsalted butter

2 tablespoons warm water (105 to 115°F.)

1½ teaspoons active dry yeast

1 teaspoon sugar

1 egg yolk mixed with ½ teaspoon water, for egg wash

3 tablespoons sesame seeds

1. Bring a large pot of water to a boil over high heat. Prepare the baking pan.

2. When the water boils, add the mushrooms and cook for about 2 minutes, just until tender. Scoop out with a slotted spoon and reserve. Slowly add the rice so the boiling does not stop, and cook until barely tender, 20 to 25 minutes.

3. Add the peas to the rice and cook for 1 to 2 minutes. Drain the peas and rice in a colander, shaking out any excess water.

4. Turn the rice mixture into a large bowl and stir in the cream cheese until melted. Let cool slightly. Stir in 2 of the eggs, 1 at a time. Stir in ⅓ cup of the Parmesan, ½ teaspoon of the salt, and ⅛ teaspoon of the pepper. Turn the mixture into the prepared pan and spread into an even layer.

5. In a large bowl, combine 1¼ cups of the sour cream with the mushrooms, 2 tablespoons of the flour, the dill, and the remaining ⅛ teaspoon pepper. Add the tuna and fold the ingredients together. Spread evenly over the rice layer. Sprinkle the hard-cooked eggs over the top. Add the olives and drizzle with 1 tablespoon of the melted butter.

6. Spoon the 2 tablespoons warm water into a small bowl or cup and sprinkle the yeast over the surface. Add the sugar and stir to dissolve. Let proof until foamy and doubled in bulk, about 5 minutes. (If this does not happen, start over with fresh ingredients.)

7. In a large bowl, combine the remaining egg with the remaining ½ cup sour cream, ½ teaspoon salt, and 2 tablespoons melted butter. Add the proofed yeast. Remove and reserve 3 tablespoons of the Parmesan; add the remaining Parmesan to the yeast and sour cream mixture along with 1 cup of the remaining flour. Beat at high speed with an electric mixer for 3 minutes (or beat vigorously, about 300 strokes with a wooden spoon). Beat in the remaining 6 tablespoons flour.

8. Spoon the batter in dollops all over the top of the casserole. Dip a spoon into cold water and evenly smooth the top of the batter; do not worry if the olives poke through. Cover loosely with a tent of aluminum foil and let rise in a warm, draft-free place until the batter has doubled in bulk, about 1 hour.

9. After the dough has risen for about 45 minutes, preheat the oven.

10. Gently brush the egg wash all over the top of the batter. Combine the sesame seeds with the reserved 3 tablespoons Parmesan and sprinkle over the top.

11. Bake in the center of the oven for 45 to 50 minutes, or until puffed and golden brown. Remove from the oven and let cool for 10 to 15 minutes. Cut into squares and serve hot or warm.

Variations: Substitute canned salmon for the tuna, first picking it over to remove the skin and bones. You can also substitute two or three 4-ounce cans of sliced mushrooms for the fresh. One-half cup sliced scallions and ½ cup chopped fresh basil can be added; omit the dill.

Reheat: If at room temperature, reheat at 350° F. for about 35 minutes; if cold, cover with foil and heat for 45 minutes. Uncover and heat 10 to 15 minutes longer.

Salmon-Potato Casserole with Broccoli

Full of dill and salmon flavor, and creamy too, this old-fashioned casserole starts with mashed potatoes and canned salmon. Since two 14-ounce cans of salmon will yield about 1 pound of boned and skinned meat, you can easily use fresh salmon to make this (see the variations). Serve with soup or salad and bread and butter.

MAKES: 6 to 8 servings

BAKES: At 350° F. for 40 to 45 minutes

CASSEROLE: Oil or butter a 13 × 9 × 2-inch casserole

3 pounds russet baking potatoes (6 large)

2 onions, chopped

2 large garlic cloves, sliced

½ cup heavy cream

1 tablespoon unsalted butter

1½ teaspoons salt

¼ teaspoon freshly grated nutmeg

⅛ teaspoon black pepper

3 large eggs

3 to 4 tablespoons snipped fresh dill, or 2 teaspoons dried

2 cans (14 ounces each) pink salmon

4 cups fresh broccoli florets (about 1 pound)

1 cup grated sharp cheddar cheese (4 ounces)

1. Peel the potatoes, cut them into 1-inch chunks, and drop them into a large pot of lightly salted water. Add the onions and garlic. Place over high heat, partially cover, and bring to a boil. Lower the heat slightly and boil over moderately high heat until the potatoes are tender, 15 to 20 minutes.

2. Drain well. Remove 2 cups of the potato chunks and reserve. Return the remaining potatoes to the pot and dry over moderate heat, shaking the pan, for about 30 seconds. Remove from the heat and stir in the cream, butter, salt, nutmeg, and pepper. Beat with a hand-held electric mixer or a potato masher until fluffy. Beat in the eggs, one at a time; beat in the dill. The mixture will be soupy.

3. Preheat the oven, and prepare the casserole. Bring a large pot of lightly salted water to a boil over high heat.

4. Pick over the salmon, breaking the meat into large chunks and removing any bones and skin. Gently fold the chunks of salmon and the reserved potato chunks into the potato mixture.

5. When the water boils, drop in the broccoli and blanch just until firm-tender, 3 to 5 minutes. Drain.

6. Spread half of the potato-salmon mixture in the pan. Scatter the broccoli florets evenly on top and press in lightly; sprinkle with half of the cheese. Carefully spread the remaining potato mixture over the top. Sprinkle on the remaining cheese.

7. Bake for 40 to 45 minutes, until golden brown on top and bubbly around the edges. Let stand for at least 10 minutes before serving.

Variations: Substitute 3 cans of drained water-packed tuna for the salmon. To make this casserole with fresh salmon, poach 1½ pounds of 1-inch-thick salmon steaks for about 10 minutes. Let cool, remove the skin and bones, and break into large chunks. To cut calories and fat, substitute milk for the cream.

Reheat: Cover the casserole with aluminum foil. If at room temperature, bake in a 350° F. oven for about 35 minutes; if cold, add 15 to 20 minutes.

Salmon-Asparagus Casserole with Parsleyed Rice

This is an elegant casserole. It's light and bright, and lovely for spring. Although it tastes best right after baking, you can prepare the rice, salmon, and asparagus well ahead, then make the sauce and bake the casserole at dinnertime.

MAKES: 4 servings

BAKES: At 450° F. for about 20 minutes

CASSEROLE: Butter or oil a 12 × 8-inch shallow casserole

1 cup long-grain white rice

1 tablespoon plus 2 teaspoons fresh lemon juice

2 tablespoons plus 1 teaspoon unsalted butter

About 1 teaspoon salt

¼ cup chopped fresh parsley

1 pound salmon fillet, sliced into medallions

12 ounces thin or medium asparagus, trimmed and cut diagonally into 2- or 3-inch lengths

2 tablespoons minced scallion bulb (white part only)

3 tablespoons all-purpose flour

1¼ cups chicken stock or canned broth, or 1 bottle (8 ounces) clam juice plus ¼ cup water

¼ cup dry white wine

2 tablespoons dry sherry

Pinch of black pepper

⅛ teaspoon freshly grated nutmeg

⅓ cup heavy cream

⅓ cup freshly grated Parmesan cheese

1. Bring a large pot of lightly salted water to a boil over high heat. Add the rice and stir until the boil returns. Boil over moderately high heat until tender but firm to the bite, 13 to 15 minutes. Drain and shake in a sieve.

2. Turn the rice into a bowl and stir in 1 tablespoon of the lemon juice, the 1 teaspoon of butter, ½ teaspoon salt, and the parsley. (The rice can be prepared a day ahead; cover and refrigerate.)

3. Preheat the oven, and prepare the casserole. Bring a large pot of lightly salted water to a boil over high heat.

4. Spread the parsleyed rice into an even layer in the casserole. Arrange the salmon medallions over the rice.

5. Drop the asparagus pieces into the boiling water and blanch until barely tender, 2 to 3 minutes. Rinse under cold water and drain well. Arrange the asparagus over the salmon.

6. Melt the remaining 2 tablespoons butter in a heavy, medium saucepan over moderate heat. Add the scallion and sauté for 1 minute. Stir in the flour and cook, stirring, for 1 to 2 minutes. The mixture will be dry. Pour in the stock, white wine, and sherry; stir constantly until slightly thickened and simmering. Add the remaining ½ teaspoon salt, pepper, and nutmeg and simmer 2 to 3 minutes. Stir in the remaining 2 teaspoons lemon juice. Remove from the heat.

7. Pour the cream into a deep bowl and beat until stiff. Fold into the hot sauce along with ¼ cup of the Parmesan. Spoon the sauce over the casserole; sprinkle with the remaining Parmesan.

8. Bake in the top third of the oven for about 20 minutes, or until deep golden brown on top. Let stand for 10 minutes before serving.

Variations: Use 2 to 3 tablespoons snipped fresh dill in place of the parsley. If desired, substitute two 14-ounce cans pink salmon, picked over to remove skin and bones and separated into large chunks. Eight ounces of sliced mushrooms, sautéed in butter, can be added.

Reheat: This casserole is best served right after baking.

Brown Rice Paella

I love the substantial, chewy quality of brown rice, and now I've discovered that I even prefer it for paella! It holds up really well and can be made ahead. I have chosen monkfish instead of lobster because it is a better bargain and has a great texture, perfectly suited for paella. Allow a couple of hours for preparing the ingredients before actually beginning to assemble this extra-special dinner-party casserole.

MAKES: 8 servings

BAKES: At 350° F. for about 40 minutes

CASSEROLE: Choose a 14-inch paella pan or 12 × 3-inch (4-quart) flame-proof casserole

2 large red bell peppers

1 large green bell pepper

½ pound sweet or hot Italian sausages (about 3 links), or firm Spanish chorizo

¼ cup water

1 cup dry white wine

1 bottle (8 ounces) clam juice

½ cup strong chicken stock or condensed broth

1½ teaspoons salt

1 teaspoon dried thyme

½ teaspoon saffron threads

2 bay leaves

2 tablespoons fresh lemon juice

8 ounces green beans, cut into 1-inch lengths

2½ cups long-grain brown rice

6 tablespoons extra-virgin olive oil

2 dozen small littleneck clams

1 pound skinless and boneless chicken thighs, cut into 1- to 1½-inch pieces (2 pounds before skinning and boning)

6 ounces smoked ham, cut into ½-inch dice (a generous cup)

1½ pounds skinless and boneless monkfish, cut into 1- to 1½-inch cubes (2 pounds before boning)

24 large to jumbo shrimp (1 to 1½ pounds), peeled and deveined

3 onions, chopped

½ cup chopped fresh parsley

2 large garlic cloves, minced

1 cup seeded, drained, and coarsely chopped canned tomatoes

1. Place the red and green bell peppers directly on the burners of a gas range or as close as possible to an electric broiler; roast, turning frequently, until charred all over. Let cool for a minute or two. Place in a plastic bag and let cool to room temperature. Rub off the skins, trim off the stems, and remove the seeds and ribs. Cut the peppers into ¾-inch squares.

2. Prick the sausages in several places and place in a medium skillet with the water. Cook over moderate heat until the water boils away. Reduce the heat and cook until well browned all over and cooked through, 25 to 30 minutes. Remove and drain on paper towels; when cool, cut into ¼-inch slices. Pour off and discard all of the fat.

3. Pour the wine into the skillet and bring to a boil over high heat. Deglaze the pan, scraping up any brown bits that cling to the bottom. Pour the mixture into a nonreactive medium saucepan.

4. Add the clam juice and chicken stock to the wine mixture. Add the salt, thyme, saffron, and bay leaves and bring to a boil. Simmer for 3 minutes. Remove from the heat and add the lemon juice; reserve.

5. Fill a 4-quart pot or dutch oven with about 3 quarts of water; bring to a boil over high heat. Add a pinch of salt and the green beans. Cook for 2 minutes from the time they hit the water. Scoop out with a slotted spoon and refresh under cold running water.

6. When the boil returns, add the rice and stir frequently until the boil returns. Partially cover and boil, stirring occasionally, for 15 minutes.

7. Drain the rice in a colander and shake out any excess water. Turn the rice into a large bowl, add 1½ tablespoons of the olive oil, and toss to coat.

8. Meanwhile, soak the clams in a large bowl of cold water for 10 minutes. Scrub thoroughly and rinse. Hold in the refrigerator until needed.

9. Spoon 1 tablespoon of the olive oil into the paella pan or casserole about 3 inches deep and place over moderately high heat. Add the chicken and brown well, without stirring, 4 to 5 minutes. Stir and cook a minute longer. Remove with a slotted spoon and reserve in a large bowl.

10. Add the sliced sausages and the ham to the pan (no more oil should be needed at this time) and sauté to lightly brown, 3 to 4 minutes. Take out and reserve with the chicken.

11. Spoon 2 tablespoons of the olive oil into the pan. Add the monkfish and shrimp and cook, tossing frequently, for 1 to 2 minutes to set. Take out and reserve with the meats. (The recipe may be prepared several hours ahead to here.)

12. Preheat the oven.

13. Spoon the remaining 1½ tablespoons oil into the paella pan and set over moderate heat. Add the onions and sauté to soften and lightly brown, about 5 minutes. Add 6 tablespoons of the parsley and the garlic; cook for 1 minute longer. Add the roasted peppers and the tomatoes. Stir up any brown bits that cling to the pan.

14. Add the rice and the green beans to the pan; toss over moderately high heat. Pour in the seasoned broth and bring to a boil. Boil, stirring occasionally, for 5 minutes. Add the reserved meats, fish, and shrimp. Fold gently to combine. The mixture should be boiling vigorously before going into the oven.

15. Bake, uncovered, for about 30 minutes.

16. Remove from the oven, stir gently to redistribute the ingredients, pushing down on the shrimp and fish. Add the clams so that the edges will open face up. Bake for about 10 minutes longer, or until the clams open.

17. Remove from the oven, cover loosely with aluminum foil, and let stand for 10 minutes before serving. Sprinkle with remaining parsley and serve hot.

Variations: Halibut, cod, swordfish, or shark can be used in place of the monkfish. One 10-ounce package of frozen peas can be used in place of the green beans; skip the blanching step. If you want to add lobster, split 4 lobster tails lengthwise and arrange, shell sides up, over the top, during the last 20 minutes. If you don't want to roast the peppers, use store-bought pimientos in place of the red peppers and sauté the green bell pepper with the onions.

Reheat: Cover loosely with aluminum foil and bake at 350° F. for 30 to 40 minutes or until hot. Sprinkle with freshly chopped parsley before serving. This casserole will taste best if not chilled. So, reheat at room temperature on the same day that it is made.

French Onion Soup

Puerto Rican Potato Casserole

Beefy Eggplant Parmigiana

Diana's Party Penne

Ravioli Casserole

Favorite Meat and Cheese Lasagne

Stuffed Polenta Casserole

Pastitsio el Greco

Mashed Potato–Stuffed Meat Loaf Casserole

Poblano-Beef Aztec Pie

Beef and Mushroom Shepherd's Pie

Cottage Casserole with Beef and Chilies

Ranch House Potato Casserole

Creamed Corn Casserole

Barbecued Pinto Beans with Kielbasa

Barbecue Baked Beans

Corned Beef and Cabbage Casserole

Pozole Casserole

Pork-and-Potatoes Casserole

Cannellini with Sausage and Mushrooms

Scalloped Potatoes with Sausage and Peppers

Black-Eyed Pea Casserole Corn Bread

Chinese Lion's Cub Casserole

Unstuffed Cabbage Casserole

| **Meats** |

Pork and Oyster Dressing

Ham and Lima Bean Casserole

Country Breakfast Casserole

Ham-Filled Potato Casserole

Party Moussaka

Lentils and Lamb Casserole

Lamb Yuvetsi

Melting Pot Casserole

French Onion Soup

Because it's got layers of cheese and bread, onion soup has always seemed like a casserole to me. It is peasant comfort food at its best. I recommend that you make the rich brown beef stock for this rather than resorting to canned broth.

MAKES: 6 side-dish servings
BAKES: At 450° F. for about 10 minutes
CASSEROLE: Choose 6 individual onion soup bowls or 1 large oven-proof tureen

1 recipe Quick Beef Stock (recipe follows)

1½ tablespoons olive oil or vegetable oil

1½ tablespoons unsalted butter

2 pounds yellow or Spanish onions (4 large), halved lengthwise and thinly sliced crosswise

1 large garlic clove, minced or crushed through a press

½ teaspoon dried thyme, crumbled

½ teaspoon salt

½ teaspoon sugar

2 tablespoons all-purpose flour

½ cup dry white wine or vermouth

¼ cup brandy or Cognac

2 tablespoons tomato paste

1 bay leaf

2 teaspoons fresh lemon juice

12 slices firm French bread, sliced diagonally ½ to ¾ inch thick

12 ounces Gruyère or other Swiss cheese, half of it grated (1½ cups) and half cut into ¼-inch-thick slices

6 tablespoons freshly grated Parmesan cheese (1½ ounces)

1. Bring the stock to a simmer. Remove from the heat and reserve.

2. Meanwhile, in a large saucepan, combine the olive oil and butter over low heat. Add the onions and sauté, stirring occasionally, until softened and lightly colored, about 20 minutes. Add the garlic, thyme, salt, and sugar. Increase the heat to moderately high and cook, stirring frequently, until the onions are caramel-colored, 20 to 30 minutes longer. If they begin to stick or seem dry, add about 2 tablespoons water and stir until it boils away. Repeat as many times as necessary to avoid scorching.

3. Stir in the flour and cook over moderate heat for 2 to 3 minutes. Pour in 1 cup of the warm stock and stir to deglaze the pan. Add the remaining stock, the wine, and brandy. Stir in the tomato paste and add the bay leaf. Bring to a boil, stirring frequently. Stir in the lemon juice. Taste for seasoning and add a pinch of salt if needed, but be careful because the cheese will contribute saltiness. Keep hot over low heat or reheat if making ahead.

4. Preheat the oven to 350°F. Arrange the slices of bread on a baking sheet and bake, turning once, until lightly toasted, about 15 minutes.

5. Move the oven shelf to the top third off the oven and increase the temperature to 450°F. Place 1 slice of toast in each of 6 soup bowls or put 6 slices in the tureen. Top each slice of toast with one slice of the cheese. Ladle in the hot soup. Place the bowls on a baking sheet. Float 1 slice of toast on top of each (or 6 in the tureen). Divide the grated Gruyère among them and sprinkle over the toast. Sprinkle with the Parmesan.

6. Bake in the top third of the oven for about 10 minutes for individual or 15 minutes for the tureen, until the cheese is bubbly and browned. Serve right away.

| Quick Beef Stock |

Instead of taking all day to make beef stock, make this quick version. It is superior to canned beef broth because it has much more flavor.

MAKES: 6 cups

1 pound ground lean beef
6 cups cold water
1 cup dry white wine
1 carrot, chopped
1 small onion, chopped

1 celery rib, chopped
1 large garlic clove, minced
1 teaspoon dried thyme, crumbled
½ teaspoon salt

1. Crumble the ground beef in a nonreactive large saucepan. Add the cold water and wine. Stir in the carrot, onion, celery, garlic, thyme, and salt. Bring to a boil over moderate heat. Partially cover and simmer gently over low heat for about 1 hour.

2. Place a sieve over a bowl and strain the mixture, pressing on the solids. Skim off the fat, or cool to room temperature, then refrigerate and lift off the fat. (If making ahead, store in a covered container in the refrigerator up to 1 week, or freeze for up to 3 months.)

Puerto Rican Potato Casserole

Inspiration for this layered beef- and olive-filled potato casserole came from the classic deep-fried *papas rellenos* (stuffed potato balls). Instead of all that fussy work and frying, you just layer the ingredients and bake them in a casserole.

MAKES: 8 servings

BAKES: At 350° F. for about 1 hour

CASSEROLE: Oil or butter a 13 × 9 × 2-inch casserole

Beef filling

2 tablespoons vegetable oil

2 tablespoons achiote (annatto) seeds

½ cup minced smoked ham (about 3 ounces)

1 large green bell pepper, trimmed and finely chopped

1 large onion, finely chopped

1 jalapeño chili, minced (partially seed, if desired, for less heat)

2 large garlic cloves, minced or crushed through a press

1½ teaspoons dried oregano, crumbled

1½ teaspoons salt

¼ teaspoon black pepper

1½ pounds lean ground beef

2 tablespoons cider vinegar

1 cup canned crushed tomatoes

½ cup sliced stuffed green olives

2 tablespoons capers, drained and chopped

1½ cups water

Cilantro mashed potatoes

4 pounds russet baking potatoes (8 large)

½ cup milk or half-and-half

2 tablespoons plus 1 teaspoon unsalted butter

1 teaspoon salt

⅓ cup chopped cilantro

½ teaspoon sweet paprika

1. Beef filling: In a small skillet or saucepan, combine the oil and achiote seeds. Place over low heat and warm gently until the oil turns bright orange and the seeds begin to sizzle, 2 to 3 minutes. Let cool to room temperature. Strain, discarding the seeds.

2. Pour the achiote oil into a nonreactive large skillet set over moderate heat. Add the ham and sauté to lightly brown, about 3 minutes. Add the bell pepper and onion, and sauté to soften, about 5 minutes. Add the jalapeño, garlic, oregano, salt, and pepper; cook for 1 to 2 minutes longer.

3. Push the vegetables to one side, increase the heat to moderately high, and crumble in the ground beef. Cook, stirring to break up the meat until the particles are fine, 3 to 4 minutes. Add the vinegar and bring to a boil. Stir in the crushed tomatoes, olives, capers, and water. Cover and simmer over low heat until the meat is very tender and the liquid is almost absorbed, about 1 hour.

4. Uncover the pan and cook until thickened, 10 to 15 minutes longer. Remove from the heat and reserve. (If making a day or two ahead, cool to room temperature, cover, and refrigerate.)

5. Preheat the oven, and prepare the casserole.

6. Cilantro mashed potatoes: Peel the potatoes and cut them into 1-inch chunks, dropping them into a large pot of lightly salted water as they are cut. Boil, partly covered, over moderately high heat, until tender when pierced with a fork, 15 to 20 minutes.

7. Drain the potatoes and return them to the pot. Shake over moderate heat for 10 seconds to dry. Add the milk, 2 tablespoons of the butter, and salt; whip with a hand-held electric mixer or mash with a potato masher. Beat in the cilantro. The mixture will be slightly stiff but will soften during baking. Assemble the casserole while the potatoes are still hot.

8. Assembly: Spread half of the hot mashed potatoes in the prepared casserole, making an even layer with a ½-inch raised edge up the sides of the casserole. Spread the beef filling into an even layer. Spread the remaining hot mashed potatoes into an even layer. (Fingers dipped in cold water will help spread the potatoes without disturbing the filling.) Dot the top with the remaining 1 teaspoon butter; sprinkle with paprika. Prick about 12 times with a fork.

9. Bake for about 1 hour, or until the top is golden brown. Let stand for 10 to 15 minutes before serving. Cut in squares and serve hot.

Variations: Lean pork or ground chicken or turkey can be used in place of the beef. The cilantro can be omitted, or ½ cup sliced scallions can replace it.

Reheat: If at room temperature, bake for 30 to 40 minutes at 350° F.; if cold, add about 15 minutes.

Beefy Eggplant Parmigiana

Well-browned egg-battered eggplant slices are layered with wine-saturated beef filling, sliced tomatoes, tomato sauce, and mozzarella and Parmesan cheeses. Make this casserole several hours, or even a day, before you plan to serve it. Choose spaghetti or another pasta and salad to serve alongside.

MAKES: 8 servings

BAKES: At 400° F. for 25 to 30 minutes

CASSEROLE: Lightly oil a 13 × 9 × 2-inch casserole

Tomato sauce

1 tablespoon olive oil

2 medium onions, chopped

1 large garlic clove, minced or crushed through a press

1 teaspoon dried oregano, crumbled

1 teaspoon dried basil, crumbled

1 can (8 ounces) tomato sauce

1 can (16 ounces) whole tomatoes

1 teaspoon salt

¼ teaspoon black pepper

Layers

4 large ripe tomatoes (2 pounds), peeled

Olive oil

1½ pounds ground lean beef

½ teaspoon salt

¼ teaspoon black pepper

1 cup dry white wine

1 large (2-pound) firm eggplant (slender but heavy for its size)

3 large eggs

2 tablespoons water

¾ cup all-purpose flour

4 cups shredded mozzarella cheese (1 pound)

1 cup freshly grated Parmesan cheese

1. Tomato sauce: Spoon the olive oil into a nonreactive medium saucepan set over moderate heat. Add the onions and sauté to soften, about 5 minutes. Add the garlic, oregano, and basil, and cook for 1 minute longer. Stir in the tomato sauce and the tomatoes, with their juices. Break up the tomatoes with a spoon and add the salt and pepper. Simmer, stirring occasionally, until slightly thickened, 20 to 30 minutes.

2. Layers: Cut out the cores of the tomatoes.

3. Spoon 1 tablespoon olive oil into a large, heavy skillet set over moderately high heat. Crumble in the ground beef and sprinkle with the salt and pepper. Cook 2 to 3 minutes, until still slightly pink. Pour in the wine and cook until it has evaporated, about 5 minutes.

4. Adjust an oven shelf to the top third of the oven. Preheat the oven and prepare the casserole.

5. With a very sharp knife, cut the eggplant crosswise into very thin (⅛- to ¼-inch) slices. In a pie pan or shallow dish, whisk the eggs with the water. Place the flour in another pie pan or shallow dish.

6. Pour ⅛ inch of olive oil into a large, heavy skillet set over moderately high heat. Regulate the heat as you brown the eggplant, keeping the oil just below the smoking point. Have the flour, egg, and eggplant slices within reach. One slice at a time, dredge the eggplant in flour, lightly coating both sides and shaking off the excess; dip into the eggs to coat, and carefully place in the hot oil. Repeat until you have a full single layer. Brown well, 3 to 4 minutes. Turn with tongs or a fork and brown the other side for 1 to 2 minutes longer. Drain on paper towels. Repeat until all the eggplant is browned, using ⅛ inch of olive oil for each batch.

7. Assembly: Arrange half of the eggplant slices overlapping slightly and covering the bottom of the prepared casserole. Thinly slice half of the tomatoes and arrange them over the eggplant. Sprinkle lightly with salt and add all of the ground beef. Top with half of the shredded mozzarella, and spoon on half the tomato sauce. Sprinkle with half the Parmesan. Repeat the layering.

8. Bake in the top third of the oven for 25 to 30 minutes, or until bubbly and golden brown. Remove from the oven and let stand for at least 15 minutes before serving. Better yet, let cool for an hour, and then reheat.

Variations: Spread the first layer of eggplant with ½ cup pesto. Mild provolone can be combined half and half with the mozzarella. Substitute ground turkey or chicken for the beef. If you want the flavor of fresh basil but don't want to make pesto, add ½ cup chopped basil leaves on top of the tomatoes.

Reheat: If the casserole is at room temperature, reheat at 350° F. for about 30 minutes; if cold, add about 15 minutes.

Diana's Party Penne

My good friend Diana Sturgis heads the test kitchen at *Food & Wine* magazine. She recently fixed this big, hearty casserole for a party. It was so good that I had a second helping, and asked her for the recipe. It's a real crowd-pleaser. I suggest that you make it for a family reunion, a covered-dish supper, or a party after a sporting event. Serve with a well-dressed salad and hot crusty Italian bread.

MAKES: 16 to 20 servings

BAKES: At 325° F. for 45 to 60 minutes

CASSEROLE: Lightly oil a 16 × 12 × 2 ½-inch roasting pan (such as an aluminum-foil turkey roaster)

4 tablespoons olive oil

2 onions, chopped

6 large garlic cloves, minced or crushed through a press

1 can (28 ounces) crushed tomatoes

1 can (28 ounces) tomato puree

2 cans (35 ounces each) whole imported Italian tomatoes in juice

1 cup chopped fresh basil

½ cup chopped fresh parsley

1 tablespoon dried oregano, crumbled

2 bay leaves

3 teaspoons salt

2 pounds ground lean sirloin

1½ cups freshly grated Parmesan cheese (6 ounces)

½ teaspoon black pepper

1 large egg

1½ pounds Italian sweet fennel sausage

2 pounds penne, preferably imported

2 pounds ricotta cheese, preferably fresh

1½ pounds mozzarella, preferably fresh, cut into ¾-inch cubes

1. Combine 2 tablespoons of the olive oil with the onions in a large flame-proof casserole or nonreactive dutch oven set over moderate heat. Sauté to soften, about 5 minutes. Add the garlic and cook for 2 to 3 minutes longer. Add the crushed tomatoes and tomato puree. Quarter the whole tomatoes and add along with all of the juices. Add ½ cup of the basil, ¼ cup of the parsley, and the oregano, bay leaves, and 2 teaspoons of the salt. Bring to a boil over moderate heat. Simmer over low heat for 30 minutes.

2. Meanwhile, in a bowl, crumble the beef and add ¼ cup of the Parmesan, ¼ cup of the basil, 2 tablespoons of the parsley, the remaining 1 teaspoon salt, the pepper, and egg. Mix thoroughly with your hands or a large spoon. Shape the mixture into firm ¾-inch balls, rolling them in your hands (if the mixture sticks, rinse your hands in cold water). Drop them into the simmering sauce as they are shaped. Simmer for about 30 minutes more after all have been added.

3. Prick the sausages all over and place in a skillet with water to almost cover. Simmer for 20 minutes; drain.

4. Return the sausages to the skillet and brown over moderate heat for about 10 minutes. Slice thinly and add to the sauce; simmer the sauce for about 15 minutes longer. (This sauce can be made a day ahead to this point. Cool to room temperature, and then cover and refrigerate.)

5. Bring a large stockpot or 2 large saucepan or dutch ovens of salted water to a boil over high heat. Add the penne and stir frequently until the water returns to a boil. Boil for about 11 minutes, until tender but firm to the bite. Drain and toss with the remaining 2 tablespoons olive oil to coat. (The pasta can be boiled a day ahead. Cool and refrigerate in large plastic bags.)

6. Preheat the oven, and prepare the roasting pan. If using a thin foil type, consider nestling two together for strength.

7. In a large pot or bowl, combine the sauce and the penne with the remaining ¼ cup basil and ¼ cup parsley. Toss to combine; remove and discard the bay leaves.

8. Turn one-third of the pasta and sauce mixture into the prepared casserole. Dot the top with tablespoon-size dollops of 1 pound of the ricotta. Scatter one-third of the mozzarella among the dollops. Sprinkle with ¼ cup of the Parmesan. Repeat the layering once more and top with the remaining one-third pasta, mozzarella, and Parmesan.

9. Bake for 45 to 60 minutes, or until hot and golden brown. Serve hot or warm.

Reheat: If at room temperature, bake at 350° F. for about 45 minutes; if cold, add about 1 cup water and reheat for 20 to 30 minutes more.

| Ravioli Casserole |

Although ravioli are usually just boiled and served with sauce, this version, inspired by lasagne, is baked in a casserole so it can be prepared in advance and served for a party. You can use fresh or frozen ravioli.

MAKES: 6 to 8 servings
BAKES: At 375° F. for 40 to 50 minutes
CASSEROLE: Coat a deep 4-quart casserole with olive oil

4 cups Tomato-Meat Sauce (page 76)

1½ pounds spinach-filled ravioli

1½ tablespoons olive oil

Parmesan sauce
2 tablespoons unsalted butter

¼ cup all-purpose flour

2 cups milk

¼ teaspoon freshly grated nutmeg

½ teaspoon salt

¼ cup dry white wine

2 large eggs

1¼ cups freshly grated Parmesan cheese (6 ounces)

3 cups shredded mozzarella cheese (12 ounces)

1. Prepare the Tomato-Meat Sauce well in advance. Make the full recipe and consider freezing half so you can make this again.

2. Preheat the oven, and prepare the casserole. Bring a large pot of lightly salted water to a boil over high heat.

3. Drop the ravioli into the boiling water and stir gently (once), partially cover the pan so the boil returns quickly. Uncover and boil gently over moderate heat (not too vigorous for ravioli or they break), stirring occasionally, until tender, 8 to 10 minutes or according to the manufacturer's directions. Drain; transfer to a large bowl and toss with the olive oil.

4. Parmesan sauce: Melt the butter in a nonreactive medium saucepan over moderate heat. Add the flour and stir with a fork for 2 minutes to cook the flour; the mixture will be dry. Pour in the milk, whisking constantly. Add the nutmeg and salt and stir until thick and simmering. Add the wine and cook, stirring, for 2 to 3 minutes longer. Remove from the heat and let cool for 10 minutes.

5. Whisk the eggs, one at a time, into the cooled sauce. Whisk in ½ cup of the Parmesan.

6. Assembly: Spread ½ cup of the Tomato-Meat Sauce in the casserole. Add half of the ravioli in an even layer. Sprinkle with half of the mozzarella shreds and ¼ cup of the Parmesan cheese. Spoon on half of the remaining Tomato-Meat Sauce and half the Parmesan sauce, drizzling it around rather than trying to spread it. Repeat the layering. Sprinkle the top with the remaining ¼ cup Parmesan.

7. Bake for 40 to 50 minutes, or until hot and bubbly. Let stand for 20 minutes before serving. This casserole is supposed to be on the saucy side so it holds up well for reheating, and for holding on the buffet table. Serve hot. Don't be fussy when serving, trying to remove whole ravioli, just dig right in with a big spoon; it looks pretty when cut into the layers of ravioli, revealing the spinach filling.

Variations: Use meat ravioli and a meatless marinara sauce. Ground chicken can be substituted for the beef in the sauce. For more fragrance and flavor, add ½ cup shredded fresh basil to the ravioli along with the olive oil.

Reheat: If the casserole is at room temperature, cover and bake at 350° F. for about 40 minutes; if cold, bake for about 1 hour. Uncover, add a little more cheese to the top, and bake for 10 to 15 minutes longer.

Favorite Meat and Cheese Lasagne

You won't find lasagne like this in Italy. It is an Italian-American development, thick and robust with meat and cheese. This pasta casserole holds up well, so it can be made ahead and reheated. In fact, you might want to cut it into portions for freezing and future reheating. Although I prefer this lasagne without any extra sauce, some of you might like to make a simple meatless tomato sauce and ladle it over the squares before reheating or serving, as many restaurants do in this country.

MAKES: 8 servings

BAKES: At 375° F. for about 1 hour

CASSEROLE: Lightly oil a 4-quart 13 × 9 × 2-inch casserole or a lasagne pan

1 recipe Tomato-Meat Sauce (recipe follows)	4 cups mozzarella cheese, grated (1 pound)
1 tablespoon olive oil	1¼ cups freshly grated Parmesan cheese (6 ounces)
1 pound lean ground round or sirloin	½ cup canned tomato sauce
1 large garlic clove, minced or crushed through a press	½ teaspoon salt
½ cup dry white wine	¼ teaspoon freshly grated nutmeg
2 cartons (15 ounces each) whole or part-skim ricotta cheese	16 curly-edged lasagna noodles (12 to 14 ounces)

1. Make the Tomato-Meat Sauce ahead.

2. Bring a large, wide pot of salted water to a boil over high heat.

3. Spoon the olive oil into a nonreactive large skillet over moderately high heat. Crumble in the ground beef and brown well, without stirring, 4 to 5 minutes. Add the garlic and cook, stirring, for 1 minute. Pour in the wine and stir until the meat is cooked and the wine evaporates, about 3 minutes. Remove from the heat and let cool.

4. Turn the ricotta into a large bowl and stir in 3 cups of the mozzarella and 1

cup of the Parmesan. Add the cooled beef, the canned tomato sauce, salt, and nutmeg. Stir to thoroughly combine the ingredients.

5. Preheat the oven, and prepare the casserole. Check the capacity of the pan to make sure it holds 4 quarts; this is important because the pan will be full.

6. Add the lasagna noodles to the boiling water and cook, stirring occasionally, until tender but firm to the bite, 10 to 12 minutes. Drain and rinse in a large bowl of cold water. The noodles can be held in cold water for up to 10 minutes. Pat dry before using.

7. Assembly: Spread ½ cup of the Tomato-Meat Sauce in the prepared pan. Arrange 4 noodles lengthwise, slightly overlapping, starting at one end. Trim a fifth noodle and fit it in crosswise at the other end to cover the bottom. Spoon on a generous 2 cups of the meat and cheese filling; top with 1¼ cups of the Tomato-Meat Sauce. Add 3 drained lasagna noodles lengthwise, not overlapping, on top. Spoon on a generous 2 cups of the filling and 1¼ cups more sauce. Repeat once more. Top with the 5 remaining noodles in the same arrangement as the first layer (4 lengthwise overlapping and 1 crosswise, trimmed to fit). Spread 1 cup of the remaining sauce over the noodles. Top with the remaining 1 cup mozzarella and ¼ cup Parmesan. Spoon the remaining ¾ cup Tomato-Meat Sauce on in dabs all over. (If you should run out of meat sauce before you get to the top, crushed canned tomatoes or tomato sauce may be used instead.)

8. Place the casserole (which will be full) on a large sheet of aluminum foil to catch any spills. Bake for about 1 hour, or until lightly browned on top and bubbly around the edges. Remove from the oven and let stand for about 20 minutes. Cut into squares and serve hot.

Variations: One cup chopped fresh basil can be stirred into the filling. Try grated Asiago or romano cheese in place of the Parmesan.

Reheat: If the casserole is at room temperature, sprinkle ¼ cup water over the top and bake at 350° F. for about 45 minutes, until hot. Uncover and bake for about 10 minutes longer. Additional cheese and tomato sauce can be added during reheating. If the lasagne is cold, add about 20 minutes more heating time.

| Tomato-Meat Sauce |

Use this for making the Favorite Meat and Cheese Lasagne on page 74 or the Stuffed Polenta Casserole on page 77. It is also mighty good with spaghetti, tortellini, and macaroni.

MAKES: About 6 cups

2 tablespoons olive oil

1 cup finely chopped onion

½ cup finely chopped celery

½ cup finely chopped peeled
   carrot

2 large garlic cloves, minced or
   crushed through a press

2 teaspoons dried oregano,
   crumbled

2 teaspoons dried basil,
   crumbled

2 bay leaves

1 pound lean ground beef

1 can (16 to 18 ounces) crushed
   tomatoes

1 cup dry white wine

1½ teaspoons salt

¼ teaspoon black pepper

1 cup water

1. Spoon the olive oil into a nonreactive large saucepan set over moderate heat. Add the onion, celery, and carrot and cook until softened, about 5 minutes. Add the garlic, oregano, basil, and bay leaves, and cook 1 to 2 minutes longer.

2. Push the vegetables to one side and crumble in the beef. Increase the heat to moderately high and cook until the meat is browned. Add the tomatoes, wine, salt, pepper, and water. Bring to a boil, then lower the heat and simmer, stirring occasionally, until thick and rich, about 45 minutes. If the sauce should become too thick, stir in a little water. Use right away, or cool to room temperature, then cover and refrigerate or freeze.

Variations: Ground chicken or turkey can be used in place of the beef. Omit the dried basil and stir in ½ cup chopped fresh basil when the sauce has cooked.

Reheat: Add a little water or wine and simmer the sauce over low heat for about 15 minutes. An extra pinch of oregano and basil will boost the flavor during reheating.

Stuffed Polenta Casserole

Although this casserole is layered like lasagne, the resemblance ends there. You make a quick-cooking polenta and simply layer it with Tomato-Meat Sauce.

MAKES: 4 to 6 servings

BAKES: At 400° F. for 35 to 40 minutes

CASSEROLE: Oil two 8-inch square pans (can be foil)

3 cups Tomato-Meat Sauce (page 76) or a commercial sauce

2 cups milk

1 cup coarse yellow cornmeal

1 teaspoon salt

1 cup cold water

2 cups grated mozzarella cheese (8 ounces)

½ cup freshly grated Parmesan or romano cheese (2 ounces)

1. Prepare the sauce ahead of time. Preheat the oven, and prepare the pans.

2. Pour the milk into a heavy, medium saucepan, preferably with a nonstick surface; place over moderate heat. Meanwhile, in a bowl, stir together the cornmeal, salt, and cold water. As the milk scalds and begins to simmer, reduce the heat to low and add the cornmeal-water mixture all at once. Stir constantly–the polenta will begin to stiffen immediately and must be stirred constantly for the first 2 minutes. Boil over low heat, beating occasionally with a wooden spoon, until very thick, about 8 minutes.

3. Working quickly, before the polenta sets, divide equally between the prepared pans. Spread evenly, and then dip your fingers in cold water and pat to even layers. Let cool to room temperature.

4. Check to see if the polenta in one pan can be easily loosened, but leave it in the pan. Spread half of the Tomato-Meat Sauce over the polenta, and sprinkle with half of the mozzarella and ¼ cup of the Parmesan. Invert the second pan of polenta over the casserole and help it fall out. Spread with ¾ cup of the remaining sauce and sprinkle with the remaining mozzarella. Spread the remaining ¾ cup meat sauce over the cheese and sprinkle with the remaining ¼ cup Parmesan.

5. Bake for 35 to 40 minutes, or until bubbly and golden brown. Let stand for 10 to 15 minutes before cutting into squares or rectangles and serving hot.

Variations: If commercially prepared polenta is available, you can cut it into ½-inch slices and arrange in layers. For a sharper flavor, replace half of the mozzarella with provolone.

Reheat: If at room temperature, bake at 350° F. for about 30 minutes; if cold, add 10 to 15 minutes more.

| Pastitsio el Greco |

My version of this famous Greek macaroni casserole is beefed up. Traditionally, this has always been an economical main course, made with little meat and lots of pasta. Not so here; I have added more meat, more cheese, and more flavor and texture. The key and crucial spicing of cinnamon plays well alongside generous doses of Greek oregano and freshly grated nutmeg. Also, both red and white wines contribute their characteristics to the final result. Since this casserole requires a good amount of work, consider making the filling a day in advance.

MAKES: 8 to 12 servings

BAKES: At 350° F. for about 1 hour

CASSEROLE: Oil a deep 4½- to 5-quart casserole or a lasagne or roasting pan (approximately 12 × 10 × 3 inches)

Meat filling

2 tablespoons olive oil

2 onions, chopped

3 large garlic cloves, minced

1 tablespoon plus 1 teaspoon dried Greek oregano, crumbled

2 pounds lean ground beef or lamb

1½ cups full-bodied dry red wine

1 can (16 ounces) crushed tomatoes

½ cup water

1 teaspoon ground cinnamon

½ teaspoon freshly grated nutmeg

1 teaspoon salt

½ teaspoon black pepper

Pasta

1 pound penne rigati, ziti, or large macaroni

1 tablespoon olive oil

Cheese sauce

4 tablespoons butter or olive oil (or half of each)

½ cup all-purpose flour

4 cups milk

½ teaspoon freshly grated nutmeg

1 cup dry white wine

½ to 1 teaspoon salt

3 large eggs, separated

16 ounces small-curd low-fat cottage cheese

2 cups grated Greek feta cheese (8 ounces)

1 cup freshly grated Parmesan cheese (4 ounces)

½ cup chopped fresh parsley

Assembly

1 cup fresh bread crumbs, toasted

1. **Meat filling:** Spoon the olive oil into a nonreactive large saucepan and place over moderate heat. Add the onions and cook until softened, about 5 minutes. Add the garlic and 1 tablespoon of the oregano; cook for 1 to 2 minutes longer.

2. Push the onions to one side of the pan and crumble in the beef. Increase the heat to high and brown, stirring occasionally, until still slightly pink, 2 to 3 minutes. Pour in the wine, stir, and let boil for 10 minutes.

3. Add the tomatoes, water, cinnamon, nutmeg, salt, and pepper; bring to a boil. Simmer, stirring occasionally, over moderately low heat until thickened, about 30 minutes. Stir in the remaining 1 teaspoon oregano. (If making ahead, let cool to room temperature; cover and refrigerate or freeze until needed.)

4. Preheat the oven, and prepare the casserole.

5. Pasta: Bring a large pot of lightly salted water to a boil over high heat. Add the pasta and cook until tender but firm to the bite, 10 to 12 minutes. Drain well. Transfer the pasta to a large bowl and toss with the olive oil.

6. Cheese sauce: Melt the butter in a nonreactive large saucepan over moderate heat. Add the flour and cook, stirring, for 2 minutes; the mixture will be dry. Off the heat, add 1 cup of the milk and the nutmeg; stir until smooth. Add the remaining 3 cups milk and cook, stirring constantly, over moderate heat until simmering and slightly thickened. Pour in the wine and add ½ teaspoon salt. Lower the heat and simmer, stirring, for 3 to 5 minutes, until slightly thicker.

7. Put the egg yolks in a medium bowl and the whites in a large deep bowl. Gradually whisk about half of the hot white sauce into the yolks. Return the mixture to the saucepan and stir over moderately low heat to cook the yolks and thicken slightly, about 2 minutes. Remove 1 cup of this sauce and stir it into the pasta. Remove the saucepan from the heat. Stir in the cottage cheese, 1¾ cups of the feta, and ¾ cup of the Parmesan. Stir in the parsley.

8. Beat the egg whites with a pinch of salt until soft mounds form. Pour in about 1 cup of the cheese sauce and fold together; add to the remaining cheese sauce and fold together. Taste and add up to ½ teaspoon salt if needed (both cheeses are salty so no more salt may be desired).

9. Assembly: Sprinkle the prepared casserole with half the toasted bread crumbs. Mix the remaining crumbs with the reserved ¼ cup feta and ¼ cup Parmesan; set aside for sprinkling on top.

10. Turn half of the macaroni into the casserole and spread into an even layer. Spoon on half of the meat filling, and pour on half of the fluffy cheese sauce. Add the remaining pasta in an even layer; spoon on the remaining meat filling. Pour on the remaining cheese sauce (if pan looks overly full, poke the handle of a wooden spoon down into the casserole in several places so the sauce can seep in). Top with the reserved cheese-crumb mixture.

11. Bake in the center of the oven for about 1 hour, or until the top is crusted golden brown and the edges are bubbly. Remove from the oven and let stand for about 20 minutes before serving.

Reheat: If the casserole is at room temperature, reheat at 350° F. for 35 to 45 minutes. If cold, sprinkle with a little water, cover with aluminum foil, and bake for 45 minutes. Uncover and bake for about 20 minutes longer, until very hot.

Mashed Potato–Stuffed Meat Loaf Casserole

This hearty, home-style meat-and-potatoes casserole combines the concept of shepherd's pie and meat loaf into a casserole. The meat loaf mixture lines the pan to form a shell and the potatoes fill the center.

MAKES: 4 to 6 servings

BAKES: At 350° F. for 50 to 60 minutes

CASSEROLE: Lightly oil an 8- or 9-inch square pan, or a shallow 2-quart casserole

Potato filling

2 pounds russet baking potatoes (4 large)

Salt

½ cup sour cream or plain yogurt

1 tablespoon unsalted butter

⅛ teaspoon black pepper

1 large egg

¼ cup chopped fresh basil, cilantro, or parsley

Meat loaf shell

1 tablespoon olive oil

2 onions, chopped

1 large garlic clove, minced or crushed through a press

1 teaspoon dried oregano, crumbled

½ teaspoon dried basil, crumbled

1 pound meat loaf mixture (a combination of equal parts ground beef, ground pork, and ground veal)

2 large eggs

½ cup plain dry bread crumbs

½ cup canned crushed tomatoes or tomato sauce

¼ cup chopped fresh basil, cilantro, or parsley

¼ cup dry white wine

1 tablespoon cider vinegar or fresh lemon juice

1 teaspoon salt

½ teaspoon celery seeds

¼ teaspoon black pepper

1 tablespoon sesame seeds or poppy seeds, or butter and paprika

1. Potato filling: Peel the potatoes, cut them into 1-inch chunks, and drop them into a large pot of water. Add a big pinch of salt and bring to a boil over moderately high heat. Partially cover, and boil until tender, 15 to 20 minutes.

2. Drain the potatoes and return them to the pot. Shake the pan for 30 seconds over moderate heat to dry. Remove from the heat; add the sour cream, butter, salt, and pepper, and beat with a hand-held electric mixer until mashed (the mixture will be dry). Add the egg and beat until fluffy. Beat in the basil.

3. Preheat the oven, and prepare the pan or casserole.

4. Meat loaf shell: Spoon the olive oil into a medium skillet over moderate heat. Add the onions and sauté to soften, 3 to 5 minutes; if dry, add 1 to 2 tablespoons water and cook a minute longer. Add the garlic, oregano, and dried basil; cook for 1 to 2 minutes longer. Turn into a large bowl and let cool about 10 minutes.

5. Crumble in the meat. Add the eggs, bread crumbs, crushed tomatoes, fresh basil, wine, vinegar, salt, celery seeds, and pepper. Mix thoroughly with your hands or a big spoon. Turn into the oiled pan and press over the bottom and up the sides of the pan to make a shell ½ to ¾ inch thick.

6. Fill the center with the mashed potato filling; sprinkle with the sesame seeds or dot with butter and sprinkle with paprika.

7. Bake for 50 to 60 minutes, or until the potato puffs up and turns golden brown. Let stand for at least 15 minutes before serving.

Variations: Use all ground beef or half ground beef and half ground chicken or turkey in place of the meat loaf mixture. When using parsley in the meat loaf shell, try adding ½ cup chopped green olives for extra flavor.

Reheat: If at room temperature, reheat, uncovered, at 350° F. for about 40 minutes, or until very hot; if cold, add about 15 minutes.

Poblano-Beef Aztec Pie

This hearty layered Mexican casserole is modeled after one that they used to serve at rooftop buffets on the terrace of the old Majestic Hotel in the colonial section of downtown Mexico City. They called it *Budín Azteca* and it is one of my favorite casseroles. Granted, it is a good amount of work, but it can be prepared well in advance of a party. Cheese and the *crema* complement the tangy tomatillos, toasted corn tortillas, and roasted chilies.

MAKES: 8 servings

BAKES: At 350° F. for 50 to 60 minutes

CASSEROLE: Lightly oil a 13 × 9 × 2-inch casserole

2 cups Salsa Verde (page 20)

1½ pounds (6 to 10 large) fresh poblano chili peppers, roasted and peeled, or 3 cans (4 ounces each) whole roasted peeled green chilies, drained

Beef filling

1 tablespoon vegetable oil

1 large onion, finely chopped

1½ pounds extra-lean ground beef

1 large garlic clove, minced or crushed through a press

1½ teaspoons dried oregano, crumbled

1½ teaspoons ground cumin

1½ teaspoons salt

¼ teaspoon black pepper

1 cup chopped drained canned tomatoes

Crema

1 cup plain yogurt

½ cup light cream

½ teaspoon salt

Layers

18 corn tortillas

Vegetable oil

1 cup sliced whole scallions

½ cup chopped cilantro

2 cups coarsely grated Monterey Jack or Muenster cheese (8 ounces)

2 cups shredded sharp cheddar cheese (8 ounces)

4 tomatoes, thinly sliced

½ cup canned tomato sauce

1. Prepare the Salsa Verde ahead. Tear the chilies lengthwise into ½-inch strips.

2. Beef filling: Spoon the vegetable oil into a nonreactive large skillet and place over moderate heat. Add the onion and sauté to soften, 3 to 5 minutes. Push to one side and crumble in the beef; increase the heat to high and brown well, 3 to 5 minutes. Add the garlic, oregano, cumin, salt, and pepper; cook for 1 to 2 minutes longer. Add the chopped tomatoes and cook until most of the liquid evaporates, about 5 minutes. Reserve.

3. Crema: In a medium bowl, stir together the yogurt, cream, and salt. Set aside at room temperature until needed.

4. Preheat the oven, and prepare the casserole.

5. Layers: Working on a plate, very lightly brush the tortillas with vegetable oil, stacking them as they are brushed (as you stack them, the underside of the tortilla you place on top of the others will be oiled by the one below).

6. Place a heavy, nonstick skillet or griddle over moderately high heat. Soften the tortillas by turning them several times on the hot surface. Cut paper towels into quarters and stack the softened tortillas between squares of paper towel.

7. In a small bowl, combine the scallions and cilantro. In a large bowl, toss together the cheeses.

8. Spread ¼ cup of the Salsa Verde in the prepared pan. Tear 6 of the tortillas into quarters and arrange them in an even layer over the salsa. Spoon half of the beef filling over the tortillas and sprinkle with half of the scallion mixture. Scatter half of the poblano strips over the scallions and spoon on ¾ cup of the Salsa Verde, interspersed with ½ cup of the crema. Arrange half of the tomato slices over all and sprinkle with one-third of the cheese mixture. Repeat once more. Tear the remaining 6 tortillas into quarters and arrange over the top.

9. Spoon the tomato sauce in swirls over the top, interspersed with swirls of the remaining Salsa Verde and crema. Scatter the remaining cheese over the top. The pan will be quite full. You should press each layer down to compact it as you assemble.

10. Place the casserole on a sheet of aluminum foil. Bake, uncovered, for 50 to 60 minutes, or until hot and bubbly and lightly browned. Let stand for at least 15 minutes before serving. Cut into squares and serve hot.

Variations: Use about 3 cups poached chicken breast, torn into wide shreds, in place of the beef, and eliminate the sautéing. Add a little chicken broth, just enough for the chicken shreds to soak it up.

Reheat: If at room temperature, reheat at 350° F. for 30 to 40 minutes. If cold, cover with aluminum foil and bake for about 1 hour. Uncover and heat for 10 to 15 minutes longer, until very hot.

Beef and Mushroom Shepherd's Pie

My good friend Reid Larrance makes a shepherd's pie like this. It's so good that I had to have the recipe for this book. But Reid cooks by instinct, not from recipes, so I concocted this from my taste memory and a conversation. It is honest meat-and-potatoes fare with a deep, complex flavor that comes from well-chosen ingredients and browning techniques. Serve it with a Caesar salad and dinner rolls with butter.

MAKES: 8 servings
BAKES: At 375° F. for 40 to 45 minutes
CASSEROLE: Lightly oil a 4-quart 13 × 9 × 2-inch baking pan or other shallow 4-quart casserole

Beef and mushroom filling

2 tablespoons olive oil

2 tablespoons unsalted butter

1½ pounds fresh mushrooms (any type), finely chopped

⅓ cup brandy or Cognac

2 onions, finely chopped

1 carrot, peeled and finely chopped

2 large garlic cloves, minced or crushed through a press

1 teaspoon ground or rubbed sage

2½ pounds extra-lean ground beef, such as sirloin or round

1½ teaspoons salt

½ teaspoon black pepper

1 teaspoon dried oregano, crumbled

1 teaspoon ground cumin

¼ teaspoon freshly grated nutmeg

½ cup all-purpose flour

1½ cups beef stock or canned broth

1 cup dry red wine

¼ cup tomato paste

2 tablespoons red wine vinegar

½ cup chopped fresh parsley

Scallion mashed potatoes

3 pounds russet baking potatoes (6 large)

⅔ cup half-and-half or milk

3 tablespoons unsalted butter

1½ teaspoons salt

¼ teaspoon freshly grated nutmeg

¼ teaspoon black pepper

1 cup thinly sliced whole scallions

¼ cup freshly grated Parmesan cheese (1 ounce)

½ teaspoon sweet paprika

1. Beef and mushroom filling: Spoon 1 tablespoon of the olive oil into a nonreactive large skillet and place over moderate heat. Add 1 tablespoon of the butter and when it melts, add all of the chopped mushrooms. Increase the heat to high and brown, without stirring, for about 3 minutes. Toss and cook for about 2 minutes longer. Averting your face, pour in the brandy and ignite. When the flames subside, cook for 2 minutes longer. Transfer to a bowl and reserve.

2. Return the skillet to moderate heat and add the remaining 1 tablespoon each of olive oil and butter. Add the onions and carrot and sauté to soften and lightly brown, about 5 minutes. Add the garlic and sage and cook for 1 to 2 minutes. Add to the mushrooms.

3. Place the pan over moderately high heat and crumble in the ground beef. Brown well, stirring occasionally, for 4 to 5 minutes. Stir in the salt, pepper, oregano, cumin, and nutmeg. Sprinkle on the flour and stir to moisten; cook for 1 to 2 minutes. Pour in the beef stock and red wine; stir in the tomato paste and vinegar. Cook, stirring, until thickened and simmering. Return the mushroom mixture to the pan and simmer for about 10 minutes to blend the flavors. Remove from the heat and stir in the parsley. (The filling can be prepared a day ahead and chilled if desired.)

4. Preheat the oven, and prepare the casserole.

5. Turn the filling into the prepared casserole.

6. Scallion mashed potatoes: Peel the potatoes and cut them into 1-inch chunks, dropping them into a large pot of lightly salted water as they are cut. Place over moderately high heat, partially cover, and boil until tender when pierced with a fork, 15 to 20 minutes.

7. Drain in a colander; return the potatoes to the pan and shake over moderate heat for 30 seconds to dry. Add the half-and-half and bring to a boil. Turn off the heat and add the butter, salt, nutmeg, and pepper; beat with a hand-held electric mixer or a potato masher until fluffy. If necessary to moisten, add a few more splashes of half-and-half. Stir in the scallions.

8. Starting at the edges of the casserole, spoon the mashed potatoes over the filling (you cannot pipe these because of the scallions). Fill in the center and use the back of a spoon to make swirls. Sprinkle with the Parmesan and paprika.

9. Place the pan or casserole on a large sheet of aluminum foil. Bake for 40 to 45 minutes, or until golden brown and bubbly. The casserole will be full and the bubbling over adds to the rustic character. Let stand for 20 minutes before serving.

Variations: To be more traditional, use lean ground lamb or half lamb and half beef. You can eliminate the scallions entirely in the mashed potatoes, or replace them with ½ cup chopped parsley, or even basil or cilantro. You can also make individual casseroles with these ingredients and they will bake up beautifully in 30 to 35 minutes.

Reheat: If at room temperature, reheat at 350° F. for about 40 minutes; if cold, reheat at 350° F. for about 1 hour.

Cottage Casserole with Beef and Chilies

Here is my beefed-up, spiced-up version of a 1950s-style American casserole. I suppose that it is a very distant cousin to lasagne, but they probably are not on speaking terms.

MAKES: 4 to 6 servings

BAKES: At 350° F. for 35 to 40 minutes

CASSEROLE: Lightly oil a 9-inch square baking pan or shallow 2-quart casserole

Tomato-beef sauce

1 tablespoon olive oil

2 onions, chopped

1 large garlic clove, minced or crushed through a press

2 teaspoons dried oregano, crumbled

1 teaspoon dried basil, crumbled

1 teaspoon salt

¼ teaspoon black pepper

1 pound extra-lean ground beef, such as sirloin or round

1 can (16 ounces) crushed tomatoes

½ cup dry white wine

Cottage cheese noodles

1 tablespoon olive oil

2 fresh jalapeño chilies (partially seeded for less heat, if desired), minced

1 large garlic clove, minced or crushed through a press

½ teaspoon dried oregano, crumbled

½ teaspoon ground cumin

½ cup low-fat plain yogurt

16 ounces small-curd low-fat cottage cheese

1 cup freshly grated Parmesan cheese (4 ounces)

½ cup sliced whole scallions

⅓ cup chopped cilantro

1 tablespoon all-purpose flour

½ teaspoon salt

¼ teaspoon black pepper

8 ounces dried medium-width (¼-inch) egg noodles

1. Tomato-beef sauce: Spoon the olive oil into a nonreactive large skillet and place over moderate heat. Add the onions and sauté until softened, 3 to 5 minutes. Add the garlic, oregano, basil, salt, and pepper and cook for 1 minute. Crumble in the ground beef, increase the heat to moderately high, and cook until well browned. Add the crushed tomatoes and wine and bring to a boil. Reduce the heat to moderate and simmer rapidly until thickened slightly, 5 to 7 minutes. Remove from the heat and reserve.

2. Adjust an oven shelf to the upper third of the oven. Preheat the oven, and prepare the casserole. Bring a large pot of lightly salted water to a boil over high heat.

3. Cottage cheese noodles: Spoon the olive oil into a nonreactive small skillet and place over moderate heat. Add the jalapeños, garlic, oregano, and cumin and sauté until the garlic is softened but not colored, about 1 minute. Stir in the yogurt, remove from the heat, and scrape into a large bowl. Stir in the cottage cheese, ½ cup of the Parmesan, the scallions, cilantro, flour, salt, and pepper.

4. Drop the noodles into the boiling water, stir once or twice, and quickly bring back to a boil. Boil the noodles for exactly 3 minutes. Drain in a colander and rinse briefly, just to cool slightly; drain well. Turn the noodles into the large bowl containing the cottage cheese mixture and toss to coat.

5. Spread half of the noodle mixture in an even layer in the prepared pan. Spoon on half of the tomato-beef sauce and sprinkle with ¼ cup of the Parmesan. Repeat.

6. Bake in the top third of the oven for 35 to 40 minutes, or until hot, bubbly, and lightly browned. Let stand for 10 minutes before serving.

Variations: You can substitute cheddar or Monterey Jack cheese for the Parmesan. Fresh basil or parsley can be substituted for the cilantro, and ground chicken, turkey, pork, or veal can be used instead of beef. You can sauté 8 ounces of sliced fresh mushrooms and add them as a filling over the first layer of noodles.

Reheat: If at room temperature, cover with aluminum foil and bake at 350° F. for about 20 minutes. Uncover and heat for 10 to 15 minutes longer. If cold, cover and reheat for 45 minutes. Uncover and heat for 10 to 15 minutes longer.

Ranch House Potato Casserole

I have a fondness for make-ahead breakfast and brunch casseroles that lighten last-minute work for morning cooks. This one combines the favorite flavors of chuckwagon cooks—bacon, cheddar cheese, onion, and bell pepper—with mashed potatoes. You can easily double this recipe and bake it in a 13 × 9 × 2-inch casserole for about 10 minutes longer.

MAKES: 4 to 6 servings

BAKES: At 400° F. for about 25 minutes

CASSEROLE: Lightly oil an 8-inch square pan or shallow 2-quart casserole

4 large (2 pounds) russet baking potatoes

3 tablespoons dry white wine or beer

1 tablespoon unsalted butter

¾ teaspoon salt

⅛ teaspoon black pepper

1 tablespoon olive oil, butter, or bacon fat

1 large green bell pepper, trimmed and cut into ½-inch squares

1 onion, chopped

½ teaspoon dried basil, crumbled

5 slices (4 ounces) bacon, fried crisp and drained

1 teaspoon cider vinegar

1 cup diced sharp cheddar cheese (4 ounces)

¼ cup shredded sharp cheddar cheese (1 ounce)

½ teaspoon sweet paprika

1. Put the whole unpeeled potatoes into a large saucepan and add cold water to cover by 1 inch. Place over high heat, partially cover, and bring to a boil. Boil over moderately high heat until tender when pierced with a fork, about 45 minutes. Drain.

2. When the potatoes are cool enough to handle, pull off the skins with the aid of a paring knife. Put them into a large bowl; add the wine, butter, salt, and pepper and coarsely mash with a potato masher or large fork.

3. Spoon the olive oil into a large, heavy skillet and place over moderate heat. Add the bell pepper, onion, and basil; sauté to soften the vegetables, about 5 minutes. Turn out over the mashed potatoes. Coarsely crumble the bacon over the mixture and stir in the vinegar. Fold in the diced cheese. (If assembling ahead of time, let the mixture cool to room temperature before adding the diced cheese. If desired, cover and refrigerate overnight; bring to room temperature before baking.)

4. Adjust an oven shelf to the top third of the oven. Preheat the oven and prepare the casserole.

5. Turn the potato mixture into the casserole and spread in an even layer. Sprinkle with the grated cheddar and the paprika.

6. Bake in the top of the oven for about 25 minutes, or until hot and golden brown. Let stand for at least 5 minutes before serving. Run a knife around the edges to loosen; cut into squares or rectangles and serve with a spatula.

Variations: You can use 1 each of medium-size red and green bell peppers, if desired. Sautéed sliced mushrooms are also a welcome addition. Also, you can substitute ½ cup diced ham or Canadian bacon for the sliced crisp bacon.

Reheat: If at room temperature, bake at 350° F. for about 25 minutes; if cold, add about 15 minutes.

| Creamed Corn Casserole |

For relaxed supper buffets, I like to make this creamy corn custard casserole hours ahead and keep it warm in a hot water bath. It is also great for brunch. Although I like this best made from fresh corn cut from the cob soon after it's been picked, it is also excellent made from frozen corn kernels.

MAKES: 6 side-dish servings

BAKES: At 350° F. for 50 to 60 minutes

CASSEROLE: Butter or oil an 8- or 9-inch casserole

6 to 8 medium ears fresh corn, or 3 cups frozen corn kernels, thawed

6 slices lean smoked bacon, chopped

1 onion, chopped

1 red bell pepper, trimmed and chopped

1 large garlic clove, minced or crushed through a press

4 large eggs

⅓ cup all-purpose flour

2 tablespoons melted unsalted butter

2 teaspoons sugar

1 teaspoon salt

¼ teaspoon black pepper

⅛ teaspoon cayenne pepper

1 cup light cream

1 cup milk

1 cup grated sharp cheddar cheese (4 ounces)

½ teaspoon sweet paprika

1 tablespoon unsalted butter, chopped (optional)

1. Preheat the oven, and prepare the pan. Choose a larger pan (such as a large roasting pan) that the square pan will fit into for a water bath.

2. Working over a large bowl, cut the corn kernels from the cobs. You will need 3 cups.

3. Place a large, heavy skillet over moderate heat. Add the bacon and stir frequently until lightly browned. Tilt the pan and spoon off all but 1½ tablespoons of the fat; leave the bacon in the pan. Add half of the corn kernels and the onion and bell pepper; sauté to soften and lightly brown, 8 to 10 minutes. Add the garlic and cook for 1 minute longer. Turn into a large bowl and let cool to room temperature.

4. Put the remaining 1½ cups corn kernels into a food processor and add the eggs, flour, melted butter, sugar, salt, pepper, and cayenne. Blend to a coarse puree. Turn into a large bowl and stir in the cream and milk.

5. Stir the grated cheese into the corn and bacon mixture. Pour in the pureed mixture and stir to combine. Turn into the prepared casserole; sprinkle with the paprika and dot with the butter, if desired.

6. Place the pan in the larger pan and add hot water to reach halfway up the sides. Bake in a hot water bath for 50 to 60 minutes, until set (a knife tip inserted in the center will come out clean). Let stand for at least 15 minutes before serving. Cut into squares and serve hot. (The casserole can be held in the water bath, in the turned-off oven, if desired, for 1 to 2 hours.)

Variations: Eliminate the bacon and sauté the corn, onion, and pepper in olive oil. For a great flavor, add 4 ounces roasted poblano chilies, cut into strips. Bake in individual ramekins for 25 to 30 minutes.

Reheat: If at room temperature, bake in a hot water bath at 350° F. for about 40 minutes; if cold, add 15 to 20 minutes.

Barbecued Pinto Beans with Kielbasa

We recently had a big family reunion at my brother Bob's home in California. Although it was a vacation for me, it was a pleasure to do most of the cooking. Something told me that this big casserole was going to become a favorite, so I took detailed notes while I put it together. We served it along-side wine-herb beef shish kebabs, barbecued chicken, potato salad, grilled vegetables, pickled cucumber slices, and fruit salad. The bacon and sausage in this dish are well browned for added flavor and then thoroughly drained of fat. By the way, pinto beans need no presoaking.

MAKES: About 24 side-dish servings
BAKES: At 325° F. for 3 hours
CASSEROLE: Lightly oil an 8- to 10-quart casserole or enameled turkey roaster

3 pounds dried pinto beans, rinsed and picked over to remove any grit	**6 to 8 large garlic cloves, minced or crushed through a press**
5 quarts plus 1 cup cold water	**1 can (16 ounces) tomato puree**
2 pounds kielbasa, cut into ½-inch slices	**1 cup cider vinegar**
1 pound sliced hickory-smoked bacon, cut into 1-inch pieces	**½ cup unsulphured molasses**
	¼ cup prepared brown mustard
3 large onions, coarsely chopped	**1 teaspoon salt**
	1 teaspoon black pepper

1. Put the beans in a large kettle or turkey roaster and pour in 4 quarts of the water. Place over 1 or 2 burners as needed and bring to a boil over high heat. Cover and simmer over low heat, stirring occasionally, until most of the water is absorbed and the beans are firm-tender, about 1 hour. Do not drain.

2. Working in batches, cook the sliced sausages in a large, heavy skillet over high heat for 4 to 5 minutes, until deep brown; turn and brown 2 to 3 minutes longer. Drain on paper towels. Pour off and discard the fat from the pan. Brown the remaining sausages. Again, discard the fat in the pan. Add ½ cup water to the pan and stir until all the browned bits clinging to the pan are dissolved. Pour into a bowl and reserve.

3. Put all of the bacon in the skillet and brown over moderate heat, stirring frequently, until crisp and golden brown, 4 to 5 minutes. Remove with a slotted spoon and drain on paper towels; add to the pot of beans. Spoon out and discard all but 2 tablespoons of the fat.

4. Add the onions and cook over moderate heat until softened, about 5 minutes. Add the garlic and cook about 2 minutes longer. Pour in the reserved pan liquid and cook a minute or two longer. Pour over the beans.

5. Add 1 quart of water to the beans and stir in the tomato puree, vinegar, molasses, mustard, salt, and pepper.

6. Preheat the oven. Transfer the bean mixture to a large casserole (unless you have cooked the beans in a roasting pan). Cover (with lid or foil) and bake for 2 hours. Uncover and add 1 cup of water. Then bake 1 hour uncovered. (If you want to make the beans ahead, cool them to room temperature after the 2-hour baking, then add water and complete baking later in the day. Or, cover and refrigerate overnight, then add the water and bake about 1½ hours the next day.)

Variations: Use small pink or red beans, but rinse and soak in plenty of cold water overnight before simmering. For a vegetarian version, sauté 6 onions in ¼ cup olive oil and omit the bacon and sausage. For a change of texture, replace 1 pound of the pinto beans with 1 pound dried large lima beans, soaked overnight, then simmered for 15 to 20 minutes, until firm-tender.

Reheat: Add 1 to 2 cups cold water and cover; if at room temperature, bake at 325° F. about 1 hour. If cold, add about 30 minutes.

| Barbecue Baked Beans |

The tangy barbecue taste of this big casserole comes from bottled barbecue sauce. Although it is very simple to put together, the casserole must bake for seven to eight hours, so plan ahead. Additional smoke flavor is contributed by a slab of hickory-smoked bacon.

MAKES: 14 cups; 14 to 20 side-dish servings
BAKES: At 250° F. for 7 to 8 hours
CASSEROLE: Choose a 4-quart flameproof dutch oven or bean pot

2 pounds dried small white beans, such as navy or pea beans, rinsed and picked over

10 cups cold water

1¼ cups bottled barbecue sauce (such as Kraft Hickory Smoke or Bull's Eye)

⅓ cup unsulphured molasses

¼ cup prepared spicy brown mustard

¼ cup packed brown sugar

1 tablespoon salt

1 large garlic clove, minced or crushed through a press

1 teaspoon dried thyme, crumbled

½ teaspoon black pepper

2 onions, peeled but left whole

1 piece (10 to 12 ounces) meaty hickory-smoked slab bacon with rind

1. Put the beans in a 4-quart flameproof casserole or dutch oven and add the water. Place over high heat and bring to a boil, stirring occasionally. Boil for 2 minutes. Turn off the heat, cover the pot, and let the beans soak for 1 hour.
2. Turn the heat to moderate, partially cover the pot, and bring to a boil, skimming any foam that accumulates on the surface; reduce the heat to low and simmer until firm-tender, 35 to 45 minutes. Do not drain.
3. Preheat the oven. Add the barbecue sauce to the beans and liquid. Stir in the molasses, mustard, brown sugar, salt, garlic, thyme, and pepper. Submerge the 2 whole onions in the mixture.
4. Using a sharp knife, score the underside of the bacon with a 1-inch grid, cutting almost through to the rind. Place on top of the casserole, rind side up.

(If the onions are floating, push them under the bacon.) Cover and bake for 3 hours.

5. Uncover and stir gently, making sure that the onions are submerged. Bake 3 hours longer.

6. Uncover the pot and bake until the top is browned, 1 to 2 hours more. If the beans should become dry at any time, add some water. When done, they should be a little on the soupy side. The beans will taste best if allowed to stand for about 1 hour before serving. As you come across the onions while serving, carefully remove and discard them.

Variations: For a simpler flavor, omit the onions, garlic, and thyme, and reduce the mustard to 2 tablespoons.

Reheat: Remove the onions and stir in about 1 cup of water. Cover and bake at 350° F. for 45 to 60 minutes; if cold, add about 20 minutes.

Corned Beef and Cabbage Casserole

Need a solution for what to do with leftover corned beef and cabbage? This hearty meat-and-potato casserole not only tastes great, it also wears a layer of greens on top. It's simple to put together because you start with leftovers.

MAKES: 6 to 8 servings
BAKES: At 350° F. for about 1 hour
CASSEROLE: Oil a 3-quart casserole

2 pounds red-skinned potatoes (6 to 8 medium) boiled with their jackets on

¼ cup all-purpose flour

2 large eggs

¾ cup milk or half-and-half

1 tablespoon Worcestershire sauce

1 teaspoon salt

⅛ teaspoon black pepper

3 cups (about 1 pound) diced (½ inch) cooked corned beef

3 cups chopped boiled green cabbage

Spinach topping

1 cup chopped cooked spinach, or 1 package (10 ounces) frozen spinach, thawed

2 large eggs

½ cup sour cream (reduced-fat is okay)

1 cup grated Swiss cheese (4 ounces)

1 tablespoon all-purpose flour

½ teaspoon salt

½ teaspoon sweet paprika

1. Preheat the oven, and prepare the casserole.

2. Peel half of the potatoes and mash them with a potato masher in a large bowl. Stir in the flour, eggs, milk, Worcestershire, salt, and pepper.

3. If desired, peel the remaining potatoes (or leave skins on); cut into ½-inch dice. Add the diced potatoes, corned beef, and cabbage; fold together. Turn the mixture into the prepared casserole; press into an even layer.

4. Spinach topping: Drain the spinach of excess liquid. Place in a large bowl and stir in the eggs, sour cream, and ¾ cup of the cheese. Stir in the flour and salt. Turn out over the filling; spread into an even layer. Sprinkle with the remaining ¼ cup cheese. Add the paprika in 2 diagonal lines.
5. Bake for about 1 hour, or until deep golden brown. Let cool for at least 10 minutes before serving.

Variations: Add ½ teaspoon caraway seeds with the corned beef. Substitute Swiss chard, kale, collard greens, or beet greens for the spinach.

Reheat: If at room temperature, bake at 350° F. for 30 to 40 minutes; if cold, add 10 to 15 minutes.

| Pozole Casserole |

Suitable for a fiesta, this oven-baked version of the classic Mexican pork and hominy stew is quite colorful when served with heaps of garnishes. I have greatly simplified the classic version by omitting the pig's head and using canned hominy in place of the dried kernels. I recommend making this at least 1 day in advance.

MAKES: 10 to 20 servings, depending on the menu
BAKES: At 325° F. for 2 hours
CASSEROLE: Choose a 6-quart casserole or dutch oven

3 pounds pork leg or shoulder, cut into 1-inch cubes

3 tablespoons vegetable oil

¼ cup all-purpose flour

6 cups chicken stock or canned broth

3 onions, chopped

3 large garlic cloves, minced or crushed through a press

1 tablespoon dried oregano, crumbled

1 tablespoon ground cumin

4 cups fresh or frozen corn kernels

1 pound fresh green beans, trimmed and cut into 1-inch pieces

2 cans (16 ounces each) yellow hominy, drained and rinsed

2 cans (16 ounces each) white hominy, drained and rinsed

2 cans (4 ounces each) whole mild green chilies, chopped

2 tablespoons cider vinegar

2 teaspoons salt

½ teaspoon black pepper

For serving

1 large head iceberg lettuce, finely shredded

3 cups sour cream at room temperature

30 radishes, thinly sliced

1 cup chopped cilantro

1 cup thinly sliced whole scallions (optional)

6 to 8 limes, cut into wedges

1. Pat the pork cubes dry. Spoon 1 tablespoon of the vegetable oil into a large, heavy skillet set over moderately high heat. Add one-third of the pork (or enough to make a single layer without crowding) and cook, without turning, until very well browned on one side, 4 to 5 minutes. Turn the pieces and brown for 2 to 3 minutes longer. Transfer to a large saucepan.

2. Spoon in ½ tablespoon more oil for each batch; brown the remaining meat in the same manner. When all of the pork has been browned and removed, add the flour and stir to moisten. Pour in 1 cup of the stock and deglaze the skillet, scraping up any brown bits that cling to the pan. Add the mixture to the pork, along with 3 cups more broth.

3. Bring the mixture to a boil. Reduce the heat to low, partially cover, and simmer until the meat is almost tender, about 1 hour.

4. Preheat the oven. Pour the pork mixture into a casserole or dutch oven.

5. Spoon the remaining 1 tablespoon vegetable oil into the skillet and set over moderate heat. Add the onions and sauté to soften, about 5 minutes; add 1 to 2 tablespoons water any time the pan seems dry. Add the garlic, oregano, and cumin, and cook for 1 to 2 minutes longer. Add to the casserole with the pork.

6. Add the corn kernels, raw green beans, yellow and white hominy, chilies, vinegar, salt, pepper, and the remaining 2 cups stock.

7. Cover the casserole and bake for 1 hour.

8. Stir, recover, and then bake for about 1 hour longer, or until the meat is very tender. If the casserole seems dry, add water. It should be slightly on the soupy side. The pozole will taste best if allowed to stand for at least 1 hour. Better yet, let cool to room temperature and then reheat. Serve hot, with the shredded lettuce, sour cream, sliced radishes, cilantro, scallions, and lime wedges.

Variations: You can use chicken thighs or breasts in place of half of the pork, but do not braise them before adding. Brown them, then add them after the casserole has baked for 1 hour.

Reheat: If at room temperature, add 1 to 2 cups water, cover, and reheat at 350° F. for about 1 hour; if cold, heat for 1½ hours.

Pork-and-Potatoes Casserole

I love the simplicity of this casserole. Although most casseroles are thick and cuttable or spoonable, this one is juicy—almost soupy. That's one of the things I like best about it. It's also a very flexible recipe and can be made with beef, pork, veal, or lamb, so be sure to check out the variations at the end of the recipe.

MAKES: 8 servings

BAKES: At 300° F. for 2 hours

CASSEROLE: Lightly oil a deep 3-quart casserole

3 pounds red-skinned or boiling potatoes (10 to 12 medium), peeled and sliced about ¼ inch thick

1 pound boneless stewing pork, cut into ¾-inch cubes

18 large whole fresh sage leaves, halved, or 1½ teaspoons ground or rubbed sage

1½ teaspoons salt

⅜ teaspoon black pepper

12 ounces fresh mushrooms, sliced

1 large or 3 small onions, chopped

2 cups beef or chicken stock or canned broth

½ cup dry white wine

1. Preheat the oven, and prepare the casserole.

2. Arrange one-fourth of the potato slices in the casserole; scatter one-third of the pork over them. Add one-third of the sage and sprinkle with ½ teaspoon salt and ⅛ teaspoon pepper. Arrange one-third of the mushrooms over the seasonings; top with one-third of the onion. Repeat the layering 2 more times. Overlap the remaining sliced potatoes on top. Press down firmly.

3. Pour in the stock and wine (it should not cover the vegetables; the mushrooms and meat will release extra juice and it will spill over if too full). Place the casserole on a sheet of aluminum foil. Cover and bake for 1 hour.

4. Uncover and bake for 1 hour longer. Let stand for 20 minutes before serving.

Variations: Replace the pork with stewing veal and use 1½ teaspoons dried thyme instead of the sage. The mushrooms can be eliminated entirely, if desired, or their flavors can be boosted considerably by adding ½ ounce dried porcini, which you have soaked in hot water for half an hour before chopping. Be sure to use the strained soaking liquid as part of the broth.

Use lamb in place of the pork and add 1 teaspoon dried rosemary in place of the sage; in addition, stir ¼ cup tomato paste into the broth before adding.

Reheat: If at room temperature, reheat at 350° F. for about 30 minutes; if cold, reheat at 350° F. for about 45 minutes.

Cannellini with Sausage and Mushrooms

White kidney beans make a favorite home-style Italian casserole. Sweet fennel-flavored Italian sausages and white wine with Italian plum tomatoes flavor them. I love this for supper with broccoli rabe and hot, crusty Italian bread with butter.

MAKES: 6 to 8 servings

BAKES: At 325° F. for about 1½ hours

CASSEROLE: Choose a deep 3-quart casserole or bean pot

1 pound dried cannellini (white kidney) beans	**2 teaspoons dried basil, crumbled**
6 cups water	**2 teaspoons dried oregano, crumbled**
1 pound sweet Italian fennel sausages	**1 teaspoon fennel seeds (optional)**
2 tablespoons olive oil	**1 cup canned crushed tomatoes**
3 onions, chopped	**1 cup dry white wine**
1 pound fresh mushrooms, sliced	**2 tablespoons red wine vinegar**
2 large garlic cloves, minced	**1½ teaspoons salt**
	¼ teaspoon black pepper

1. Rinse the beans and pick over to remove any grit. Put them in a large (3-quart) heavy saucepan with 5 cups of the cold water and bring to a boil over high heat. Boil for 2 minutes. Cover, turn off the heat, and let soak for 1 hour.

2. Return the beans to a boil over high heat. Partially cover and simmer over low heat until firm-tender, 20 to 30 minutes. Do not drain.

3. Meanwhile, prick the sausages 10 or 12 times all over with a fork. Place in a heavy medium skillet and add ¼ cup water. Cook over moderate heat, turning occasionally, until the water boils away and the sausages begin to sizzle. Lower the heat and cook until well browned, 20 to 30 minutes. Drain on paper towels and let cool. Cut into ¼-inch-thick slices.

4. Preheat the oven.

5. Spoon the olive oil into a nonreactive large skillet and place over moderate heat. Add the onions and sauté to soften and lightly brown, about 5 minutes. Add the mushrooms, increase the heat to high, and brown, adding 1 to 2 tablespoons water if dry. Stir in the garlic, basil, oregano, and fennel seeds; cook for 1 to 2 minutes longer. Add the sausages, tomatoes, wine, vinegar, salt, pepper, and 1 cup water. Bring to a boil. Transfer to a large bowl. Add the beans, with their simmering liquid, and toss.

6. Turn the mixture into the casserole or bean pot. Bake uncovered for about 1½ hours, or until the beans are tender. If dry at any time, add a little water. Serve hot.

Variations: To use great northern beans in place of the cannellini, cook in 6 cups of water and simmer for 45 to 60 minutes before adding to the casserole. After the casserole has baked, ¼ cup chopped fresh basil can be added just before serving.

Reheat: Stir in about ½ cup water. Cover and bake at 350° F. for about 45 minutes. If cold, add about 15 minutes.

Scalloped Potatoes with Sausage and Peppers

This great home-style casserole combines the flavors of scalloped potatoes with Italian sausages and peppers. It's a good wintertime supper dish.

MAKES: 8 to 10 servings
BAKES: At 375° F. for about 1¼ hours
CASSEROLE: Butter or oil a large oval gratin (about 11 × 16-inch) or other shallow 4- to 4½-quart casserole

1 pound sweet Italian fennel sausages

2 onions, halved lengthwise and thinly sliced crosswise

2 red bell peppers, trimmed and cut into ¼-inch-wide strips

2 medium green bell peppers, trimmed and cut into ¼-inch-wide strips

2 to 3 large garlic cloves, minced

2 teaspoons fresh rosemary, or 1 teaspoon dried

2 teaspoons dried oregano, crumbled

2 teaspoons dried basil, crumbled

3 pounds red-skinned boiling potatoes (6 large), peeled

1½ teaspoons salt

⅜ teaspoon black pepper

6 tablespoons all-purpose flour

2 cups half-and-half

1 cup milk

¼ cup freshly grated Parmesan cheese

1. Place a large, heavy skillet over moderately high heat. If using sausages in casings, slit the casings lengthwise and peel off. Crumble the meat into the hot pan and sauté until no longer pink, 3 to 5 minutes. Tilt the pan and spoon off and discard all but 1 tablespoon of the fat.

2. Add the onions and bell peppers and sauté to soften, adding 1 to 2 tablespoons water if dry, about 10 minutes.

3. Stir in the garlic, rosemary, oregano, and basil and cook for 1 to 2 minutes longer. Reserve.

4. Preheat the oven, and prepare the gratin dish or casserole.

5. Cut the potatoes into ¼-inch-thick slices as you assemble the dish. Arrange one-fourth of the potatoes in the casserole. Sprinkle with ½ teaspoon salt and ⅛ teaspoon pepper. Spoon on one-third of the sausage and pepper mixture and sprinkle with 2 tablespoons of the flour. Repeat the layering 2 more times. Top with the remaining potatoes. Pour the half-and-half and milk over.

6. Cover tightly with aluminum foil. Bake for 45 minutes.

7. Uncover and spoon some of the cream over the top and sprinkle with the Parmesan. Bake, uncovered, for about 30 minutes longer, or until deep golden brown and bubbly and the potatoes are tender when pierced. Let stand for at least 20 minutes before serving.

Variations: You can lighten this casserole by using all milk in place of the half-and-half, or make it richer by using light cream or heavy cream.

Reheat: If at room temperature, bake uncovered at 350° F. for about 45 minutes. If cold, cover and reheat at 350° F. for 30 minutes. Uncover and bake for about 30 minutes longer, until steaming hot.

Black-Eyed Pea
Casserole Corn Bread

Here is a meaty, moist casserole corn bread that's rich with breakfast sausage (sautéed and well drained) and black-eyed peas. It's amazing, but the flavor of the peas comes through in every bite. This side dish can be served for breakfast, lunch, brunch, or supper. You might serve it with a soup or stew, or with scrambled eggs or an omelet.

MAKES: 8 to 12 side-dish servings
BAKES: At 350° F. for about 45 minutes
CASSEROLE: Butter or oil a 13 × 9 × 2-inch casserole

3 tablespoons vegetable or olive
  oil or melted butter

1 onion, chopped

12 ounces bulk breakfast
  sausage

1 garlic clove, minced

1 fresh jalapeño chili, minced,
  or ¼ teaspoon cayenne
  pepper (optional)

1 cup drained canned black-
  eyed peas

¾ cup canned cream-style corn

2 tablespoons cider vinegar or
  white vinegar

1 teaspoon salt

1 cup low-fat plain yogurt

2 large eggs

1 cup coarse yellow cornmeal

1¼ cups grated sharp cheddar
  cheese (5 ounces)

¾ cup all-purpose flour

½ teaspoon baking powder

½ teaspoon baking soda

½ teaspoon sweet paprika

1. Preheat the oven, and prepare the casserole.

2. Spoon 1 tablespoon of the oil into a large, heavy skillet and place over moderate heat. Add the onion and sauté to soften, 3 to 5 minutes. Turn out into a large bowl.

3. Crumble the sausage into the pan and sauté over moderately high heat to brown; stir frequently to break up any big clumps. Tilt the pan and spoon off the fat. Return the pan to the heat and add the garlic and jalapeño; sauté for 1 minute longer. Turn out over the onions and let cool for 5 minutes.

4. Add the black-eyed peas, corn, vinegar, and salt to the onion and sausage mixture. Toss and let cool to room temperature.

5. Stir the yogurt, eggs, and 2 tablespoons oil into the mixture to blend. Add the cornmeal and 1 cup of the cheese. Stir to combine.

6. In a small bowl or on a sheet of waxed paper, stir together the flour, baking powder, and baking soda. Add to the mixture and stir just to blend. Quickly turn the mixture into the prepared pan and spread out in an even layer. Sprinkle the top with the remaining ¼ cup cheese and the paprika.

7. Bake for about 45 minutes, or until a toothpick inserted into the center is clean when pulled out, and the edges begin to pull away from the sides of the pan. Let cool for 15 to 20 minutes before serving. Cut into squares. Refrigerate any leftovers, covered with plastic wrap.

Variations: Turkey sausage can be used in place of the pork sausage. Use lean ground pork in place of the sausage, adding about ½ teaspoon ground or rubbed sage with the garlic. Or, use lean ground beef instead of sausage and pink or black beans (rinsed and drained) in place of black-eyed peas. Add ½ teaspoon ground cumin and ½ teaspoon oregano when sautéing the beef.

Reheat: If at room temperature, reheat at 350° F. for about 20 minutes, or until hot; if cold, add about 15 minutes.

Chinese Lion's Cub Casserole

Chinese cooks don't make many casseroles, but Lion's Head is one of their classics. Traditionally, it is made as giant meatballs and reserved for banquets (as a show-off dish, because of the high cost and huge amount of meat used). I have made the meatballs smaller and more manageable, and combined them with rice and napa cabbage so everything bakes together to make a one-dish supper. By the way, the frilly napa cabbage surrounding the meatballs is said to represent the lion's mane.

MAKES: 4 to 6 servings
BAKES: At 325° F. for 1¼ to 1½ hours
CASSEROLE: Lightly oil a deep 3-quart casserole

1 small (2 pounds) head napa
   cabbage

1 pound lean ground pork

3 whole scallions, minced

1 tablespoon plus 2 teaspoons
   grated fresh ginger

2 tablespoons soy sauce

½ cup plus 1 tablespoon dry
   sherry

1 teaspoon Oriental sesame oil

½ teaspoon Chinese five-spice
   powder

1 tablespoon vegetable oil

1 cup long-grain white rice

1 cup chicken stock or canned
   broth

½ teaspoon salt

2 to 3 slices smoked bacon,
   halved

1. Preheat the oven, and prepare the casserole.
2. Cut the head of cabbage in half lengthwise. Cut out the core and discard. Cut lengthwise into 3 or 4 wedges, then crosswise into 1½-inch pieces. Drop the cabbage into a large pot of lightly salted boiling water set over high heat. Partially cover and cook for 2 minutes, stirring occasionally. Drain and reserve.
3. In a large bowl, combine the ground pork, scallions, 2 teaspoons of the ginger, the soy sauce, 1 tablespoon of the sherry, the sesame oil, and the five-

spice powder. Finely chop 1 cup of the cabbage and add it to the bowl. Mix thoroughly with your hands.

4. Spoon the vegetable oil into a medium skillet set over moderate heat. Add the rice and stir until toasted golden brown, 4 to 5 minutes. Add 1 tablespoon ginger and cook for 1 minute. Pour in the stock, the remaining ½ cup sherry, and the salt. Boil 3 minutes over moderately high heat. Remove from the heat.

5. Arrange half of the remaining blanched cabbage in the casserole. Spoon on half the rice mixture.

6. Using a ¼-cup measure, scoop out portions of the meat mixture and roll into balls (there will be 12 to 14). Arrange the balls over the rice. Spoon on the remaining rice mixture and top with the remaining cabbage. Arrange the bacon over the cabbage. Cover and bake 1¼ to 1½ hours, or until the rice is tender and the liquid is absorbed. Uncover and let stand for 15 minutes before serving.

Variations: Soak 8 large dried shiitake mushrooms in warm water for 30 minutes. Drain and cut off stems. Slice the caps into ¼-inch slivers and add to the casserole with the rice. Four ounces of coarsely grated fresh mushrooms can be added to the meat mixture for flavor and texture.

Reheat: This casserole is best eaten on the same day that it is made. To reheat the casserole (at room temperature), cover and bake at 350°F. for 30 to 40 minutes, until hot.

Unstuffed Cabbage Casserole

The inspiration for this easy layered casserole was the Hungarian-style stuffed cabbage rolls that my mother made frequently during my childhood. I just took all of the same ingredients and layered them to make it simple to assemble. This is a casserole that gets better upon reheating, so consider making it early in the day that you plan to serve it or even a day ahead.

MAKES: 8 servings
BAKES: At 350° F. for 1½ hours
CASSEROLE: Choose a 13 × 9 × 2-inch glass or ceramic casserole

1 large (3½-pound) head green cabbage

¾ cup long-grain white rice

¾ pound lean ground beef

¾ pound lean ground pork

2 large eggs

2 cans (8 ounces each) tomato sauce

1 tablespoon sweet paprika

1½ teaspoons dried basil, crumbled

2½ teaspoons salt

½ teaspoon black pepper

1 cup water

1. Quarter the head of cabbage through the core (the core portion will be attached to the quarters and hold the leaves together). Choose a large pot that will hold all 4 pieces and half-fill with water. Cover and bring to a boil over high heat. Add the cabbage, partially cover, and boil until tender, about 15 minutes. Drain and let cool slightly.

2. Bring about 2 quarts of water to a boil in a large saucepan over high heat. Gradually add the rice so the boil does not stop and boil until firm-tender, about 12 minutes. Drain in a sieve and shake out any excess water. Turn the rice into a large bowl and let cool for 10 minutes.

3. Crumble in the ground beef and pork. Add the eggs and 1 can of the tomato sauce. Add the paprika, basil, salt, pepper, and ½ cup water. Mix thoroughly with your hands or a large spoon.

4. Preheat the oven.

5. In a bowl, combine the remaining can of tomato sauce with the remaining ½ cup water. Spread ½ cup of the diluted tomato sauce in the bottom of the glass or ceramic baking dish (tomato and cabbage tend to react with metals).

6. Slice off and discard the core portion of each cabbage quarter. Peel off all of the largest outer leaves (there will be 6 or 7 from each quarter). Finely chop enough of the heart of the cabbage to measure about 2 cups lightly packed.

7. Begin lining the casserole with the largest leaves, overlapping them all around the sides of the pan so the wide ends are on the bottom of the pan, the leaves run up the sides, and the points hang over the sides (these will be folded inward over the casserole later). Fill in the bottom of the casserole with a double layer of leaves. Spoon in half the meat mixture and spread into an even layer. Add all of the chopped cabbage and press lightly. Spoon ½ cup of the diluted tomato sauce over the chopped cabbage. Spoon on the remaining meat and pat to make an even layer. Arrange the remaining leaves over the top; fold in the overhanging leaves all around. The casserole will be full. Prick all over with a long fork–about 50 times. Spread the remaining diluted tomato sauce over the top.

8. Cover with a sheet of parchment or waxed paper; top that with a sheet of aluminum foil and crimp the edges tightly all around. Place on a sheet of aluminum foil to catch any spills. Bake in the center of the oven for 1½ hours. Remove from the oven and let stand, covered, for 30 minutes before serving. Cut into 8 squares and serve hot, spooning some of the juices from the casserole over each portion.

Variations: Use brown rice instead of white; the parboiling until firm-tender will take about 30 minutes. All beef can be used, or half beef and half ground turkey or chicken is also suitable.

Reheat: If at room temperature, cover and bake at 350° F. for 40 to 50 minutes. If cold, pour ¼ cup water over the top. Cover as before, and reheat for 1¼ hours.

| Pork and Oyster Dressing |

This dressing works so well as a casserole because there are juices from the oysters to add richness and flavor.

MAKES: 8 to 10 side dish servings
BAKES: At 325° F. for 40 to 45 minutes
CASSEROLE: Butter or oil a 2½- to 3-quart casserole

3 tablespoons olive oil

3 tablespoons unsalted butter

4 cups coarsely chopped onions

3 cups finely diced celery

2 large garlic cloves, minced

5 cups toasted croutons

1 pound lean ground pork

1 cup chopped fresh parsley

1 teaspoon rubbed sage

1 teaspoon ground cumin

1 teaspoon dried basil

½ teaspoon freshly grated nutmeg

1½ teaspoons salt

¼ teaspoon black pepper

2 dozen (1 pint) raw oysters, with ⅓ cup of the liquor reserved

3 large eggs

Chicken broth, if needed

1. Preheat the oven to 325° F.

2. Combine the olive oil and butter in a large, heavy skillet over moderate heat. Add the onions, celery, and garlic, and sauté to soften and lightly brown, 10 to 15 minutes. Turn into a large bowl. Add the croutons and toss.

3. Crumble the ground pork over the bread mixture. Add the parsley, sage, cumin, basil, nutmeg, salt, and pepper. Coarsely chop or quarter the oysters and add them. In a bowl, whisk the eggs with the oyster liquor. Gradually add to the dressing, tossing to absorb evenly. If the dressing is too dry, add a little more oyster liquor. If it is too wet, add a spoonful of dried bread crumbs.

4. Turn the dressing into the prepared casserole. Cover and bake for 40 to 45 minutes, until browned. Check after 30 minutes and if it seems dry, spoon a little chicken broth over the top and continue baking.

Reheat: Sprinkle ¼ cup water over casserole and cover. If at room temperature, bake at 350° F. for about 30 minutes; if cold, add about 15 minutes.

Ham and Lima Bean Casserole

My mother used to make something like this and it has been one of my favorite casseroles for most of my life. It is hearty, soupy, and substantial–a fine casserole to make when there's leftover ham. At other times, a ham steak works perfectly well. By the way, dried lima beans require no soaking, and they cook quickly.

MAKES: About 10 cups; 6 to 8 servings
BAKES: At 325° F. for about 1¼ hours
CASSEROLE: Choose a 3-quart flameproof casserole, such as a dutch oven

1 pound dried large lima beans, rinsed and picked over

5 cups cold water

2 tablespoons olive oil

2 cups diced ham (½ inch)

2 onions, coarsely chopped

2 large garlic cloves, minced or crushed through a press

2 teaspoons dried basil, crumbled

1 teaspoon dried thyme, crumbled

1 cup strong chicken stock or condensed canned broth

One can (28 ounces) whole tomatoes

½ teaspoon salt

1. Combine the lima beans with the cold water in the casserole. Place over moderate heat and bring to a boil, stirring occasionally. Lower the heat and simmer, partially covered, until the beans are plump and most of the liquid has been absorbed, about 30 minutes.

2. Preheat the oven. Spoon 1 tablespoon of the olive oil into a medium skillet set over moderately high heat. Add the ham and sauté until brown, 4 to 5 minutes. Turn out over the lima beans. Spoon the remaining 1 tablespoon olive oil into the skillet and add the onions. Sauté over moderate heat to soften and lightly color, 4 to 5 minutes, adding 1 to 2 tablespoons water if dry. Add the garlic, basil, and thyme, and cook 1 to 2 minutes. Pour in the stock and stir to loosen brown bits on the bottom of the skillet. Add the juices to the lima beans.

3. Place a sieve over a bowl and drain the tomatoes. Cut in half crosswise and gently squeeze out the seeds. Coarsely chop the tomatoes and add to the casserole along with ½ cup of the strained tomato juice and the salt. Bring to a boil.

4. Cover the casserole and bake for 45 minutes.

5. Uncover the casserole, stir gently, and bake until the beans are tender and the top is browned, about 30 minutes longer. The casserole should be slightly soupy.

Variations: Smoked chicken or turkey can be used in place of the ham. Or, omit the ham and add about 6 slices of bacon, cut into 1-inch pieces and browned. If desired, fresh tomatoes can be used in place of canned, and ¼ cup shredded fresh basil can be substituted for the dried, but add after removing the casserole from the oven.

Reheat: If at room temperature, reheat at 350° F. for about 45 minutes; if cold, add 15 minutes.

Country Breakfast Casserole

This hearty sausage, cheese, and egg casserole fits into one of my favorite casserole categories, the make-ahead main-dish brunch casserole. For a real Southern country menu, include grits (either plain or the Brewsky Cheese Grits on page 175), Virginia country ham, bourbon apples, fresh fruit, sour cream coffee cake with pecans, coffee, and perhaps bubbly mimosas. Since you assemble this casserole the night before, all you do is pop it into a hot oven the next morning.

MAKES: 8 servings

BAKES: At 350° F. for 50 to 60 minutes

CASSEROLE: Butter or oil a 13 × 9 × 2-inch casserole

12 slices firm white homemade-style white bread (such as Pepperidge Farm), crusts trimmed and slices cut into 1-inch squares

1½ pounds bulk breakfast sausage

2 cups grated sharp cheddar cheese (8 ounces)

12 large eggs

2 teaspoons dry mustard

4 cups milk

1½ teaspoons salt

½ teaspoon sweet paprika

1. The night before or at least 8 hours before you want to bake this casserole, prepare the casserole. Arrange the bread in two even layers in the casserole.

2. Place a large skillet over moderately high heat. Crumble in the sausage and cook to lightly brown. Turn into a sieve set over a bowl and drain the pork; discard the fat. Spoon the sausage over the bread; sprinkle with the cheddar cheese.

3. In a large bowl, whisk the eggs with the mustard; whisk in the milk and salt. Ladle the egg mixture into the casserole. Cover and refrigerate overnight.

4. Preheat the oven. Uncover the casserole and sprinkle with the paprika. Bake for 50 to 60 minutes, or until puffy, well browned, and set. Let stand for 10 minutes before serving.

Variations: Use Italian sausage in place of breakfast sausage and sliced Italian semolina bread in place of the sliced white bread. You can also add a layer of sautéed peppers and onions and replace the cheddar with 1 cup each of grated Parmesan and mild provolone.

Reheat: This is best served right after baking. If the baked casserole is at room temperature, reheat at 350° F. for about 45 to 55 minutes; if cold, add about 15 minutes.

Ham-Filled Potato Casserole

Sliced potatoes are sandwiched with a light ham filling and seasoned with a wisp of clove along with Oriental seasonings of ginger and sesame. A creamy white sauce naps the top while grated Parmesan creates a golden brown crust. This is the perfect recipe for leftover ham.

MAKES: 8 servings

BAKES: At 350° F. for about 1 hour

CASSEROLE: Butter or oil a 13 × 9 × 2-inch casserole

Ham filling

1 pound boneless ham, coarsely chopped

1 large egg

1 tablespoon Oriental sesame oil

1 tablespoon minced fresh ginger

½ teaspoon salt

⅛ teaspoon black pepper

⅛ teaspoon ground cloves

1 cup milk or half-and-half (or a combination)

½ pound ground lean pork

Potato layers

3 pounds (8 to 12 medium) red-skinned boiling potatoes

2 tablespoons chopped fresh parsley

White sauce

2 tablespoons unsalted butter

¼ cup all-purpose flour

2 cups milk

1 teaspoon salt

⅛ teaspoon black pepper

⅛ teaspoon freshly grated nutmeg

¼ cup freshly grated Parmesan cheese (1 ounce), for topping

1. Preheat the oven, and prepare the casserole. Bring a large pot of lightly salted water to a boil over high heat.

2. Ham filling: In a food processor, combine the ham, egg, oil, ginger, salt, pepper, and cloves. Process to grind. Add the milk and ground pork and process to finely grind.

3. Potato layers: Peel the potatoes, cut them in half lengthwise, then cut them crosswise into ¼-inch slices (if doing this more than 5 minutes ahead, keep in cold water until ready to cook). Drop into the boiling water, cover the pot, and return the water to a boil. Cook for 3 minutes after the boil returns. Drain.

4. Arrange half of the potatoes in the prepared casserole, slightly overlapping them to cover the bottom. Sprinkle with the parsley. Spread the ham filling over all without disturbing the potatoes. Dip your fingers in cold water and pat the mixture into an even layer. Starting at the edge of the casserole, arrange potato slices on top of the ham filling so the flat edges butt up against the side of the casserole all around. Slightly overlap the remaining potato slices over the top to cover the filling.

5. White sauce: Melt the butter in a medium saucepan over moderate heat. Stir in the flour and cook for 1 to 2 minutes. Add 1 cup of the milk and stir until smooth. Add the remaining 1 cup milk, the salt, pepper, and nutmeg; stir or whisk constantly until thick and simmering. Lower the heat and simmer for 2 to 3 minutes, or until very thick.

6. Spoon the sauce over the potatoes, coating all of the slices. Sprinkle on the Parmesan.

7. Bake for about 1 hour, or until golden brown on top and bubbly around the edges. Let stand for 10 minutes. Cut into squares and serve hot.

Variations: Peel 1 sweet potato and thinly slice; arrange the slices all over the ham filling before topping with the second white potato layer. The ginger and sesame oil can be omitted from the recipe.

Reheat: Cover the casserole with aluminum foil. If at room temperature, reheat in the top third of a 350° F. oven for about 45 minutes. Uncover, increase the temperature to 425° F., and bake for about 10 minutes longer to brown the top slightly. If the casserole is cold, add 10 to 15 minutes.

Party Moussaka

This is the kind of fun cooking project that I love for a Sunday morning. There's something wonderful about cooking big on Sundays. Maybe it's just because my mother always cooked wonderful things for Sunday dinner, and the house was full of fragrance from morning till night.

My version of Greek moussaka is made from the robust earthy layers of potato, eggplant, and zucchini, and is filled with tender slices of lamb and tomato, topped with *Saltsa Aspri* (creamy cheese sauce). The flavors get bigger and better if made four to six hours ahead, so make this well in advance. Refrain from adding more salt, even if it seems to need more—moussaka seems to become saltier upon resting.

MAKES: 8 to 12 servings
BAKES: At 375° F. for 45 to 60 minutes
CASSEROLE: Lightly oil a 15 × 10 × 2-inch baking dish, lasagne pan, or disposable aluminum roasting pan

Vegetables

2 pounds red-skinned or all-purpose potatoes (4 large)

2 pounds zucchini

2 pounds small to medium eggplants

Salt

Olive oil

Lamb filling

2 tablespoons unsalted butter

3 onions, chopped

3 large garlic cloves, minced or crushed through a press

1½ pounds lean well-trimmed boneless leg of lamb or shoulder, thinly sliced across the grain and cut into 1-inch squares

2 teaspoons dried oregano, crumbled

½ teaspoon dried thyme, crumbled

2 teaspoons salt

½ teaspoon coarsely ground black pepper

1 can (28 ounces) whole peeled tomatoes, with their juices

¼ cup plain dry bread crumbs

¼ cup chopped fresh parsley

1 large egg, lightly beaten

Saltsa Aspri

3 tablespoons unsalted butter

2 tablespoons olive oil

½ cup all-purpose flour

4 cups milk

½ teaspoon freshly grated
nutmeg

1 teaspoon salt

¼ teaspoon coarse black
pepper

1 cup freshly grated Parmesan
cheese or Greek *Kephalotýri*
(4 ounces)

Assembly

¼ cup plain dry bread crumbs

2 large eggs, lightly beaten

1. **Vegetables:** Put the potatoes in a medium pot and add cold water to cover generously. Place over moderately high heat, partially cover, and bring to a boil. Cook until tender when pierced with a fork, 30 to 40 minutes. Drain and let cool.

2. Meanwhile, trim both ends from the zucchini and eggplants. Cut the zucchini crosswise into slices slightly thicker than ¼ inch; cut the eggplant crosswise into slices about ½ inch thick.

3. Arrange the eggplant slices on a large rack and sprinkle very lightly with salt. Let stand for 15 minutes.

4. Turn the eggplant slices and sprinkle very lightly with salt. Let stand for about 30 minutes longer. Wipe off the salt and moisture with paper towels.

5. Place a large, heavy skillet over moderately high heat and pour in a scant ¼ inch of olive oil. When very hot, add a layer of zucchini and brown until deep golden brown, about 3 minutes; turn and brown lightly, about 1 minute longer. Drain on paper towels. Brown all of the zucchini. Add a little more olive oil, increase the heat to high, and brown the eggplant in the same manner. (Eggplant soaks up oil at the beginning and then releases some of it after browning and even more during draining.) Brown all of the eggplant, adding olive oil as needed. Drain on paper towels.

6. **Lamb filling:** Melt the butter in a large, heavy skillet or dutch oven over moderately high heat. Add the onions and sauté to soften and lightly brown, about 5 minutes. Add the garlic and cook for 1 minute longer. Add the lamb and stir briefly; cook over high heat until no longer pink, about 3 minutes. Add the oregano, thyme, salt, pepper, and tomatoes (with their juices).

Break up the tomatoes with a spoon and bring the mixture to a boil. Reduce the heat to low, cover, and simmer for 15 minutes.

7. Uncover, increase the heat to moderate, and cook for about 15 minutes longer to reduce some of the liquid. Remove from the heat; set aside to cool for 15 to 20 minutes.

8. Stir the bread crumbs, parsley, and egg into the filling.

9. Preheat the oven, and prepare the baking dish or pan.

10. Saltsa Aspri: Combine the butter and olive oil in a medium saucepan over moderate heat. As soon as the butter melts, stir in the flour and cook for 1 to 2 minutes; the mixture will be dry. Whisk in the milk. Add the nutmeg, salt, and pepper and cook, stirring frequently, for about 3 minutes, until the sauce thickens and simmers. Remove from the heat and stir in the Parmesan. Let cool for 5 to 10 minutes.

11. Assembly: Sprinkle the bread crumbs in the prepared baking dish. Peel the potatoes, if desired, and cut into ¼-inch slices. Arrange all of the slices in an even layer in the pan. Spread with half of the lamb filling. Arrange all of the eggplant slices in an overlapping layer. Spread on the remaining lamb filling. Arrange all of the zucchini in an even layer. Whisk the eggs into the *Saltsa Aspri*; pour the sauce over to cover the moussaka.

12. Bake for 45 to 60 minutes, or until golden brown and bubbly. Let cool in the pan on a rack for at least 20 minutes before serving. Reheat at 350° F. for about 15 minutes, or until hot. Cut into large squares and serve hot.

Variations: Use sliced roast beef in place of the lamb, or use ground lean lamb or beef in place of sliced meat. The potato slices can be browned in olive oil, if desired.

Reheat: If at room temperature, reheat at 350° F. for 30 to 40 minutes. If cold, cover with aluminum foil and reheat at 350° F. for about 1 hour. Uncover and heat for 10 to 15 minutes longer.

Lentils and Lamb Casserole

This healthy and nutritious casserole, with its deep, complex flavors, is substantial fare suitable for supper, lunch, or dinner.

MAKES: 8 servings

BAKES: At 350° F. for about 1½ hours

CASSEROLE: Choose a deep 4-quart covered casserole

2 pounds lean well-trimmed boneless leg of lamb, cut into 1-inch cubes

3 tablespoons vegetable oil

4 cups chicken stock or canned broth

1 cup water

3 cups coarsely chopped onions

1½ cups coarsely chopped celery

1½ cups coarsely chopped carrots

4 large garlic cloves, minced or crushed through a press

3 bay leaves

1 tablespoon dried oregano, crumbled

1 teaspoon dried rosemary, crumbled

1 pound fresh mushrooms, sliced

1 can (28 ounces) whole tomatoes

1 cup dry white wine

1 pound dried lentils, rinsed and drained

2 teaspoons salt

1. Pat the lamb dry with paper towels. Spoon 1 tablespoon of the oil into a large sauté pan or skillet over moderately high heat. When very hot, add half the lamb and sauté, stirring, until very deep brown, about 5 minutes (use a splatter screen, if available). Turn and brown the meat about 2 minutes longer. Transfer the meat to a medium saucepan. Spoon 1 tablespoon more oil into the skillet, brown the remaining lamb, then add to the saucepan.

2. Pour 1 cup of the stock and the water into the saucepan. Cover and simmer the lamb over low heat until tender, 45 minutes to 1 hour.

3. Preheat the oven.

4. Spoon the remaining 1 tablespoon oil into the pan used to brown the lamb. Place over moderate heat and add the onions, celery, and carrots; cook until softened and brown, 7 to 10 minutes, adding 1 to 2 tablespoons water each time pan seems dry. Add the garlic, bay leaves, oregano, and rosemary. Cook 2 to 3 minutes. Add the mushrooms, increase the heat, and toss until softened, 2 to 3 minutes longer.

5. Stir in the tomatoes, with their juice, and break up with a spoon or chop. Add the remaining 3 cups stock, the wine, lentils, and salt. Add the lamb and stir frequently until the mixture boils. Simmer 5 minutes, stirring frequently.

6. Turn the mixture into the casserole. Cover with a lid or double layer of aluminum foil, and bake for 45 minutes. Remove the casserole from the oven and fold gently with a large spoon to turn the ingredients from the bottom to the top. If the casserole seems dry, add a little more water. Cover, return the casserole to the oven, and bake an additional 45 minutes. Remove the bay leaf and serve.

Variations: This casserole can be made with lean stewing beef, but the initial cooking of the meat will take slightly longer. The mushrooms can be omitted.

Reheat: Add ½ to 1 cup water and cover. If at room temperature, bake at 350° F. for about 45 minutes; if cold, bake about 1 hour, or until very hot.

| Lamb Yuvetsi |

The Greek word *yuvetsi* names both the casserole dish and the food cooked in it. Although it can contain any kind of pasta along with meat or vegetables, most often it is made from orzo and lamb, as it is here. In Greece, cooks put the casserole together and take it to the town's communal oven to bake. Serve this with sliced cucumbers and yogurt on the side.

MAKES: 12 cups; 8 servings

BAKES: At 325° F. for about 40 minutes

CASSEROLE: Choose a heavy 4-quart flameproof casserole or dutch oven

2 pounds lean well-trimmed boneless lamb (leg or shoulder), cut into 1-inch cubes

3 tablespoons vegetable oil

2 medium onions, chopped

3 large garlic cloves, minced

1 tablespoon dried Greek oregano, crumbled

1 teaspoon dried thyme, crumbled

1 3-inch cinnamon stick

5 whole cloves

1 teaspoon salt

2½ cups dry white wine

1 can (28 ounces) whole tomatoes, with juice

4 cups chicken stock or canned broth

1 pound orzo (rice-shaped pasta)

1 cup water

2 tablespoons fresh lemon juice

¼ teaspoon black pepper

½ to ¾ cup chopped fresh mint

1. Pat the lamb cubes dry with paper towels. Spoon 1 tablespoon of the vegetable oil into a large, heavy skillet and place over moderately high heat. Add half the lamb and brown very well (use a splatter screen, if available), 4 to 5 minutes. Turn the pieces and brown the other side about 2 minutes. Take out and transfer to the casserole or dutch oven. Spoon 1 tablespoon more oil into the skillet and brown the remaining lamb in the same manner. Transfer to the casserole.

2. Spoon the remaining 1 tablespoon oil into the skillet and add the onions; cook over moderate heat to soften, 3 to 5 minutes. Add the garlic, oregano, thyme, cinnamon stick, cloves, and salt; cook about 1 minute longer. Pour in 2 cups of the wine and bring to a boil, stirring up any brown bits on the bottom of the pan.

3. Turn the mixture into the casserole. Add the tomatoes with their juice and break up with spoon, and bring to a boil over moderate heat. Lower the heat, partially cover, and simmer gently until the meat is tender but not falling apart, about 1 hour. Remove and discard the cinnamon stick (and the cloves if you see them).

4. Preheat the oven. Pour the chicken stock into a medium saucepan and bring to a boil over high heat. Add the orzo and stir until the liquid returns to a boil. Lower the heat and cook, partially covered, until the broth is absorbed and the orzo is almost tender, about 10 minutes, stirring occasionally.

5. Turn the orzo into the casserole. Stir to combine, cover tightly, and bake for 20 minutes. Remove from the oven, uncover, and add the water along with the remaining ½ cup wine, lemon juice, and pepper. Cover and bake about 20 minutes longer, until the meat and orzo are very tender. If at any time the casserole is too dry (it should be neither soupy nor dry), add a little water. Remove from the oven and let stand, covered, about 10 minutes before serving. Serve in shallow soup plates, sprinkled with fresh mint.

Variations: Beef can be used in place of lamb; chuck or bottom round would be good choices, though the initial 1 hour simmer may need to be extended slightly to tenderize the beef. Parsley can be used in place of mint, or combined with the mint.

Reheat: To my taste, this casserole is best fresh; however, if you want to make it ahead add 1 to 1½ cups water and cover. If at room temperature, bake at 325° F. for about 45 minutes; if cold, bake about 1 hour, or until very hot, stirring once or twice.

| Melting Pot Casserole |

Here is my favorite flexible formula for making a casserole from what's on hand: You can use any kind of pasta you have around (I often combine three or four shapes to make use of odds and ends in my cupboard) and any variety of meat that might be leftover–pork, lamb or beef, roast turkey or chicken. While you're at it, throw in any green vegetable from the freezer or crisper drawer. All you do is make a white sauce and layer everything in a casserole.

MAKES: 4 servings

BAKES: At 375° F. for 40 to 45 minutes

CASSEROLE: Lightly oil a shallow 2-quart casserole or 8- or 9-inch square pan

8 ounces elbow macaroni, penne, ziti, shells, or other pasta, or a combination (even spaghetti or fettuccine, broken into 2-inch pieces)

1½ tablespoons olive oil

1 teaspoon dried oregano, crumbled

1 teaspoon dried basil, crumbled

1 teaspoon salt

1 onion, finely chopped

1 large garlic clove, minced

1 fresh jalapeño chili, minced, or ¼ teaspoon dried red pepper flakes or cayenne pepper (optional)

¼ teaspoon dried thyme

1½ to 2 cups diced (½ inch) cooked lean pork, beef, lamb, ham, chicken, or turkey

2 tablespoons unsalted butter or olive oil

¼ cup all-purpose flour

2 cups milk

1 cup grated cheese, such as Fontina, provolone, Swiss, or cheddar (4 ounces)

1 can (8 ounces) tomato sauce

1 to 2 cups cooked chopped spinach, Swiss chard, broccoli, zucchini, or green cabbage

2 tablespoons dry bread crumbs or cracker crumbs

1. Preheat the oven, and prepare the casserole or baking pan.

2. Drop the pasta into a large pot of lightly salted boiling water over high heat. Stir until the boil returns and then frequently until the pasta is tender but firm, 10 to 12 minutes. Drain. Transfer to a large bowl and toss with ½ tablespoon of the olive oil. Add the oregano, basil, and ½ teaspoon of the salt and toss again.

3. Spoon the remaining 1 tablespoon olive oil into a large skillet over moderate heat. Add the onion and sauté to soften, 3 to 5 minutes. Add the garlic, hot pepper, thyme and ½ teaspoon salt; sauté for 1 minute longer. Add the meat, increase the heat, and lightly brown for 2 to 3 minutes.

4. Melt the butter in a medium saucepan over moderate heat. Stir in the flour and cook, stirring, for 1 minute; the mixture will be dry. Pour in the milk and stir over moderate heat until thickened and simmering. Lower the heat and simmer, stirring occasionally, for 2 to 3 minutes longer. Remove from the heat and stir in the cheese until melted.

5. Spoon one-third of the pasta into the prepared casserole. Top with half of the meat. Spoon on ⅓ cup of the tomato sauce. Add half of the cooked vegetables and one-third of the cheese sauce. Repeat the layering once more. Top with the remaining pasta. Drizzle the remaining tomato sauce over the top; sprinkle on the remaining cheese and the bread crumbs.

6. Bake for 40 to 45 minutes, or until golden brown on top and bubbly around the edges. Serve hot.

Reheat: If at room temperature, bake at 350° F. for about 30 minutes; if cold, add about 15 minutes.

Bean and Cheese Casserole Dip

Chile Relleno Casserole

Black Bean Tamale Pie

Cheddared Summer Squash Casserole

Green Beans Almendrado

Zucchini-Poblano Casserole

Southwestern Hominy Casserole

Roasted Ratatouille Casserole

Fragrant Fennel Casserole

Wild, Brown, and White Rice Pilaf

Brown Rice Casserole with Spinach Filling

Almond Rice Pilaf

Two-Potato Casserole

Potato-Gorgonzola Casserole

Tangy Cheddar Potato Casserole

Potato-Cheddar Kugel

Roasted Red Pepper and Potato Casserole

Spinach, Mushroom, and Potato Oven Omelet

Mashed Potato–Broccoli Casserole

Potato-Porcini Casserole

Bow Tie Four-Cheese Casserole

Tortellini in Creamy Roquefort Sauce

Meatless Main & Side Dishes

Wisconsin Lasagne

Artichoke Lasagne with Tomato-Basil Sauce

Brewsky Cheese Grits

Parmesan Spoon Bread

Swiss Cheese Fondue

Bean and Cheese Casserole Dip

I bake this in a colorful, hand-painted Mexican *cazuela* and put it out with corn chips for casual parties.

MAKES: 12 to 24 appetizer servings
BAKES: At 375° F. for 30 to 40 minutes
CASSEROLE: Lightly oil a 2-quart casserole

3 cans (16 ounces each) pinto beans, drained, rinsed, and drained again

1 package (8 ounces) cream cheese

1½ cups grated sharp cheddar cheese (6 ounces)

1 can (8 ounces) tomato sauce

1 to 2 teaspoons hot pepper sauce or minced jalapeño

½ teaspoon ground cumin

1 teaspoon salt

¼ teaspoon black pepper

1 can (4 ounces) whole mild green chilies, drained and chopped

Corn chips, for serving

1. Preheat the oven, and prepare the casserole.

2. In a food processor, combine two-thirds of the beans with the cream cheese and 1¼ cups of the cheddar. Add the tomato sauce, hot pepper sauce, cumin, salt, and pepper. Process to a smooth puree.

3. Turn the puree into a large bowl and stir in the remaining whole beans and the green chilies. Transfer to the prepared casserole and sprinkle with the remaining ¼ cup cheddar. Bake for 30 to 40 minutes, or until hot and bubbly. Serve hot from the casserole with corn chips.

Variations: Monterey Jack cheese can be used in place of the cheddar and canned crushed tomatoes in place of the tomato sauce.

Reheat: Cover the casserole. If at room temperature, reheat at 350° F. for 30 to 35 minutes; if cold, give it 10 to 15 minutes longer.

Chile Relleno Casserole

Chiles rellenos are stuffed chili peppers. They are one of my favorite Mexican dishes, but are a little fussy to make. Here I have combined all of the flavors and textures of a good chile relleno, but layered them in a casserole. I urge you to make this with fresh-roasted poblanos; if they are not available, use canned whole mild green chilies.

MAKES: 6 servings

BAKES: At 350° F. for 35 to 40 minutes

CASSEROLE: Lightly oil a shallow 12 × 8-inch casserole

2 pounds poblano chilies (8 to 12), or 4 cans (4 ounces each) whole peeled green chilies, drained

1 tablespoon olive oil or vegetable oil

1 onion, chopped

1 large garlic clove, minced or crushed through a press

½ teaspoon dried oregano, crumbled

½ teaspoon ground cumin

4 large eggs

1 large package (8 ounces) cream cheese, softened

½ cup milk

⅓ cup chopped cilantro

¼ cup all-purpose flour

1 teaspoon salt

1½ pounds ripe tomatoes (2 large beefsteak or 6 medium), halved, cored, and sliced crosswise ¼ inch thick

1 cup grated sharp cheddar cheese (4 ounces)

1 cup grated Monterey Jack cheese (4 ounces)

½ cup sliced whole scallions

1. Roast the poblano chilies by placing them directly in the flame of a gas burner turned to high, or about 3 inches below an electric broiler. Turn them frequently until blistered and charred all over. Let them cool for a minute or two, then place in a plastic bag and let cool to room temperature. Rub away the skin with your fingers or work over a colander under gently running water. Slit the peppers and scrape out the seeds. Cut off the stems and cut the peppers into 2-inch squares.

2. Preheat the oven, and prepare the casserole.

3. Spoon the oil into a medium skillet and place over moderate heat. Add the onion and sauté to soften, about 3 minutes. Add the garlic, oregano, and cumin; sauté for 1 minute longer. If the mixture seems too dry, add 1 table-spoon water.

4. In a food processor or blender, combine the eggs, cream cheese, milk, cilantro, flour, and salt; blend until smooth.

5. Arrange half of the poblanos in the baking dish; top with half of the tomato slices. Spoon on the onion mixture in an even layer. Scatter ¾ cup each of the cheddar and Monterey Jack cheeses over the onion. Sprinkle with the scallions. Pour half of the egg mixture over all. Arrange the remaining poblanos on top, and then layer with the remaining tomato slices. Pour on the remaining egg mixture and top with the remaining ¼ cup each of cheese.

6. Bake for 35 to 40 minutes until deep golden brown and bubbly around the edges. Remove from the oven and let stand for 10 to 15 minutes before serv-ing. Cut into squares and serve hot.

Variation: Add sliced pitted black olives or whole corn kernels on top of the tomatoes.

Reheat: Cover with aluminum foil. If at room temperature, bake at 350° F. for 25 to 30 minutes; if cold, add 10 to 15 minutes.

Black Bean Tamale Pie

Here is one of my all-time favorite vegetarian dishes. It is substantial and so satisfying you won't miss the meat. The key is marinating the black beans in sherry and lemon juice before layering.

MAKES: 6 to 8 servings
BAKES: At 350° F. for about 1 hour
CASSEROLE: Lightly oil a 13 × 9 × 2-inch casserole

3 cans (16 ounces each) black beans, rinsed and drained

½ cup dry sherry

2 tablespoons fresh lemon juice

2 tablespoons olive oil

3 cups fresh or thawed frozen corn kernels

1 fresh jalapeño chili, minced with the seeds

1 large garlic clove, minced or crushed through a press

1½ teaspoons ground cumin

1 teaspoon dried oregano, crumbled

2 teaspoons salt

¼ teaspoon black pepper

5¼ cups water

1½ cups peeled, seeded, and coarsely chopped tomatoes (fresh or canned)

1 cup sliced whole scallions

½ cup chopped cilantro

2 cups coarse yellow cornmeal

1½ cups low-fat plain yogurt

2 cups coarsely grated sharp cheddar cheese (8 ounces)

½ cup canned tomato sauce

For serving (optional)

Sour cream

Black olives

Radishes

Cilantro sprigs

1. In a sealable plastic bag or shallow dish, combine the black beans, sherry, and lemon juice. Marinate in the refrigerator 2 to 12 hours. Drain before using.
2. Spoon the olive oil into a large heavy nonstick or well-seasoned skillet over moderately high heat. Add the corn, toss once, then let brown very well, about five minutes. Toss again and continue browning for a minute or two. Add the jalapeño, garlic, cumin, oregano, ½ teaspoon of the salt and the pep-

per. Cook a minute or two, then pour in ¼ cup of the water to deglaze the pan. Turn out into a large bowl and toss in the tomatoes, scallions, and cilantro. The recipe may be prepared a day ahead to here.

3. Preheat the oven, and prepare the casserole.

4. Bring 3 cups of the water and the remaining 1½ teaspoons salt to a boil in a large, heavy saucepan over high heat. Meanwhile, in a medium bowl, stir together the cornmeal and remaining 2 cups cold water. Add the cornmeal mixture to the boiling water and stir constantly until the mixture returns to a boil. Reduce the heat to low and cook, stirring frequently, until the mixture is as thick as mashed potatoes, about 5 minutes. Stir in 1 cup of the yogurt. Cook over very low heat, stirring frequently, until again as thick as mashed potatoes, about 8 minutes.

5. Spread about two-thirds of the cornmeal batter in the prepared casserole (keep the remainder covered over hot water to keep warm), making a 1-inch raised edge all around. Spoon the drained black beans on top and press in lightly. Sprinkle 1½ cups of the cheese over the beans. Add all of the corn-tomato mixture and spread into an even layer. Spoon the remaining cornmeal mixture over the top in dabs and spread to make an even layer that covers the top (it's okay if some of the vegetables show through).

6. Spoon the remaining yogurt and the canned tomato sauce in alternating diagonal lines. Sprinkle with the remaining ½ cup cheddar.

7. Bake about 1 hour, or until deep golden brown on top. Remove from the oven and let stand for at least 15 minutes before serving. Cut into squares, remove them with a spatula, and serve hot, with a dollop of sour cream, a couple black olives and radish slices, and a sprig of cilantro, if desired. If making ahead, cool to room temperature, cover with foil, and refrigerate.

Variations: To make a meaty version, add about 2 cups shredded cooked chicken on top of the beans and use chicken stock in place of the 3 cups of boiling water. (Stick with cold water for moistening the cornmeal.) You can also use sautéed ground beef with the beans.

Reheat: Sprinkle the casserole with 2 to 3 tablespoons water and cover with foil. If at room temperature, bake at 350°F. for about 45 minutes; if cold, add about 15 minutes.

Cheddared Summer Squash Casserole

Here is a colorful vegetable side dish that you can really sink your teeth into. It combines the slender green zucchini and the bright yellow crookneck squash that are first the darlings and then the dominators of the summer vegetable garden.

MAKES: 6 to 8 side-dish servings
BAKES: At 350° F. for about 30 minutes
CASSEROLE: Butter or oil a shallow 12 × 8-inch casserole

1 pound zucchini (3 to 4), cut into ¼-inch-thick rounds

1 pound yellow crookneck or summer squash (3 to 4), cut into ¼-inch-thick rounds

1 tablespoon unsalted butter

¼ cup plain dry bread crumbs

2 large eggs, separated

1 cup sour cream

2 tablespoons all-purpose flour

½ teaspoon salt

1½ cups grated sharp cheddar cheese (6 ounces)

1. Bring a large pot of salted water to a boil over high heat. Meanwhile, preheat the oven, and prepare the casserole. Drop the squash into the water, partially cover, and let the water return to a boil. Cook until the squash is barely tender, 2 to 3 minutes. Drain in a colander, and then on several layers of paper towels until needed.

2. Melt the butter in a small skillet set over low heat. Add the bread crumbs and toss to coat.

3. Arrange half of the squash slices, slightly overlapping, in a layer in the casserole, alternating yellow and green squash.

4. In a medium bowl, whisk the egg yolks until smooth. Add the sour cream and flour, and whisk to blend.

5. In a large bowl, whisk or beat the egg whites until stiff. Stir a spoonful of the whites into the sour cream mixture to lighten it. Pour the lightened mixture over the beaten whites and fold together with a rubber spatula.

6. Sprinkle ¼ teaspoon of the salt over the squash layer in the casserole.

Spoon on half of the egg mixture, and lightly spread into a layer. Sprinkle with half of the cheese. Repeat the layering. Top with the buttered crumbs.

7. Bake about 30 minutes, until golden brown on top and bubbly around the edge. Let stand for at least 5 minutes before serving.

Variations: For a Southwestern flavor, add roasted, peeled, chopped green poblano chilies, or 1 or 2 cans (4 ounces each) chopped mild green chilies. For a smoky accent, fry 5 or 6 slices of hickory-smoked bacon, and crumble them over the cheese layers.

Reheat: If at room temperature, reheat at 350° F. for about 25 minutes; if cold, bake for 40 to 45 minutes.

Green Beans Almendrado

With a nippy cheddar cheese flavor and creamy consistency, this casserole is a good choice as a side dish for vegetarian menus and with roasted poultry and meat.

MAKES: 6 to 8 side-dish servings
BAKES: At 350° F. for 25 to 30 minutes
CASSEROLE: Lightly oil a shallow 12 × 8-inch casserole

2 pounds tender, fresh green beans, cut on the diagonal into 2 or 3 pieces

2½ tablespoons butter

½ cup slivered almonds (2 ounces)

¼ cup all-purpose flour

2 cups milk

1 tablespoon cornstarch

¼ cup dry white wine

1 teaspoon Dijon mustard

½ teaspoon Worcestershire sauce (optional)

¼ teaspoon Tabasco sauce

1 teaspoon salt

⅛ teaspoon black pepper

1½ cups grated sharp cheddar cheese (6 ounces)

1 small package (3 ounces) cream cheese, cut up

1. Preheat the oven, and prepare the casserole.

2. Drop the green beans into a large pot of lightly salted boiling water set over high heat. Partially cover and cook until tender, 5 to 7 minutes. Drain.

3. Melt ½ tablespoon of the butter in a small skillet set over moderate heat. Add the almonds and toast until golden, stirring occasionally, 3 to 4 minutes. Reserve for topping.

4. Melt the remaining 2 tablespoons of butter in a large saucepan set over moderate heat. Stir in the flour and cook, stirring, until lightly colored, 1 to 2 minutes. The mixture will be dry. Pour in the milk and stir until smooth. Bring the sauce to a simmer and cook to form a medium-thick white sauce.

5. In a small bowl, stir together the cornstarch and wine until smooth. Add to the sauce and stir over low heat until very thick, about 1 minute. Stir in the mustard, Worcestershire sauce, Tabasco sauce, salt, and pepper. Add the cheddar cheese and the cream cheese. Stir over very low heat until smooth and melted, about 1 minute. Remove from the heat. Add the green beans and toss to coat. Turn into the prepared casserole and top with the toasted almonds. Bake for 25 to 30 minutes, or until lightly browned on top and bubbly around the edges. Let stand for 10 minutes before serving.

Variations: When yellow wax beans are available I like to use half yellow beans mixed with the green beans. For a smoky flavor, add 1 cup chopped smoked ham with the green beans.

Reheat: If at room temperature, bake uncovered at 350°F. for 20 to 25 minutes; if cold, add 10 to 15 minutes.

Zucchini-Poblano Casserole

The wonderful deep flavor of roasted mild poblano chilies permeates this layered casserole, built over a base of cilantro rice.

MAKES: 8 servings

BAKES: At 350° F. for 50 to 60 minutes

CASSEROLE: Butter or oil a 13 × 9 × 2-inch casserole

1 pound poblano chilies (6 medium), or 2 cans (4 ounces each) roasted, whole green chilies, rinsed and drained

1½ pounds zucchini (4 to 6), sliced on the diagonal ½ inch thick

1½ cups long-grain white rice

1 cup cold water

2 tablespoons olive oil

1½ teaspoons salt

⅓ cup chopped cilantro

2 large tomatoes (1 pound), sliced ¼ inch thick

¼ teaspoon black pepper

3 cups shredded Monterey Jack cheese (12 ounces)

2 cups sour cream (reduced-fat is okay)

1 teaspoon dried oregano, crumbled

1 teaspoon ground cumin

½ cup sliced whole scallions

¼ cup chopped fresh parsley

1 teaspoon sweet paprika

1. Roast the chilies by placing them directly in the flame of a gas burner turned to high, or 2 to 3 inches below an electric broiler. Turn frequently until blistered and blackened all over. Let cool for 2 to 3 minutes. Enclose in a plastic bag and let cool to room temperature.

2. Rub the skins away and slit the peppers lengthwise. Pull out the seeds and ribs; cut out the stems. Cut the peppers into 1-inch squares.

3. Preheat the oven, and prepare the casserole. Bring 2 large pots of lightly salted water to a boil over high heat. Drop the zucchini into one and cover. When the boil returns, cook for 1 minute; drain and reserve.

4. Slowly add the rice to the other pot, so boiling doesn't stop, and boil, stirring once or twice, for 8 minutes. Add the cold water to stop the boiling, then drain in a sieve, shaking out any excess water.

5. Turn the rice into a large bowl and add the olive oil, ½ teaspoon of the salt, and the cilantro; toss to combine. Turn into the prepared casserole and pat into an even layer.

6. Arrange the poblanos over the rice followed by the zucchini and tomatoes. Sprinkle with ½ teaspoon of the salt and the black pepper. Scatter 2 cups of the cheese over the tomatoes.

7. In a bowl, stir together the sour cream, oregano, cumin, scallions, parsley, and the remaining ½ teaspoon salt. With a wooden spoon handle or a finger, poke about 12 holes through the layers in the casserole. Spread the sour cream mixture over the top and sprinkle with the remaining 1 cup cheese and the paprika.

8. Bake the casserole for 50 to 60 minutes, or until bubbly and golden brown. Remove from the oven and let cool for about 15 minutes. Cut into squares and serve hot.

Variations: Brown rice can be used in place of white: Start with about 3 quarts of boiling water, and boil the rice for about 30 minutes, or until tender but firm to the bite. Half yellow summer squash and half sharp cheddar can be used for half of the zucchini and half of the Monterey Jack cheese.

Reheat: If at room temperature, bake at 350°F. for 35 to 40 minutes; if cold, add about 20 minutes.

Southwestern Hominy Casserole

Hominy are giant corn kernels–the kind used to make pozole–that have been dried, soaked, cooked, and hulled. But, you can start with canned hominy, as in this simple-to-put-together old-fashioned Southwestern side-dish casserole. Serve it with burgers, broiled salmon, or roasted or barbecued meat.

MAKES: 6 to 8 side-dish servings

BAKES: At 325°F. for 35 to 40 minutes

CASSEROLE: Oil a shallow 12 × 8-inch casserole or gratin dish

1 cup low-fat plain yogurt

½ cup sour cream

½ teaspoon hot pepper sauce (optional)

1 can (4 ounces) whole mild green chilies, drained and chopped

2 tablespoons all-purpose flour

1 teaspoon salt

½ teaspoon dried oregano, crumbled

½ teaspoon ground cumin

¼ teaspoon black pepper

2 cans (16 ounces each) yellow hominy, rinsed and drained again

1 can (16 ounces) pink beans, rinsed and drained again

½ cup grated sharp cheddar cheese (2 ounces)

½ cup grated Monterey Jack cheese (2 ounces)

½ teaspoon sweet paprika

1. Preheat the oven, and prepare the casserole or gratin dish.

2. In a large bowl, stir together the yogurt, sour cream, and hot pepper sauce. Add the chilies, flour, salt, oregano, cumin, and pepper; stir to combine. Stir in the hominy and beans.

3. Toss together both cheeses; stir half of it into the mixture. Turn into the prepared casserole and sprinkle with the remaining cheese and the paprika. Bake for 35 to 40 minutes, or until lightly browned and bubbly around the edges. Serve hot.

Variations: Eight ounces of poblano chilies can be roasted, peeled, seeded, and chopped in place of the canned green chilies for a fresher, bigger flavor. White hominy, or 1 can each of white and yellow hominy, can be used. Kidney beans, black beans, or pinto beans can be used in place of the pink beans. For more flavor and a fancier presentation, serve sprinkled with chopped cilantro and sliced scallions.

Reheat: Cover the casserole with aluminum foil. If at room temperature, reheat at 325°F. for about 30 minutes; if cold, add 10 to 15 minutes.

Roasted Ratatouille Casserole

One of my favorite summer vegetable side dishes is ratatouille–the French eggplant, zucchini, onion, and bell pepper concoction that is bathed in olive oil. Here I have turned it into a cold casserole that tastes best when made ahead of time. This makes a big casserole, so you can cook one day and eat all week–or serve a crowd for a casual party.

MAKES: 14 to 20 side-dish servings
BAKES: At 325° F. for 1½ hours
CASSEROLE: Coat a deep 4½- to 5-quart casserole with olive oil

6 large red or yellow bell peppers (2 pounds), preferably a combination

¾ cup extra-virgin olive oil

6 to 8 onions (2 pounds), coarsely chopped

5 large garlic cloves, minced or crushed through a press

3 firm eggplants (1 pound each), cut into 1-inch cubes

6 to 8 zucchini (2 pounds), quartered lengthwise and cut into 1-inch chunks

3 cups peeled, seeded, chopped tomatoes (fresh or canned)

¼ cup tomato paste

1 tablespoon coarse (kosher) or sea salt

½ teaspoon black pepper

5 large sprigs fresh oregano, or 1 tablespoon dried

5 large sprigs fresh thyme, or 2 teaspoons dried

1 large sprig fresh rosemary, or 1 teaspoon dried

½ cup chopped fresh basil leaves

¼ cup chopped fresh parsley

1. Roast the bell peppers by placing them directly in the flame of a gas burner turned to high, or 3 inches below an electric broiler. Turn frequently until blistered and blackened all over. Let cool 1 to 2 minutes. Place in a plastic bag and let cool to room temperature.

2. Rub the skins away and cut out the stems. Halve and pull out the seeds and ribs. Cut the peppers into 1-inch squares.

3. Adjust an oven shelf to the top third of the oven and preheat to 500° F.

4. Spoon 3 tablespoons of the olive oil into a large, heavy sauté pan set over moderate heat. Add the onions and cook until softened and lightly brown, 8 to 10 minutes. Add the garlic and cook for 2 minutes longer, stirring.

5. Lightly oil a large, shallow pan. Add all of the cubed eggplant and toss with ¼ cup of the remaining olive oil. Roast on the top shelf of the oven about 15 minutes, or until well browned.

6. Turn the cubes of eggplant with a large spoon and roast for about 10 minutes longer. Remove from the oven; reduce the oven temperature to 325°F.

7. Meanwhile, drop the zucchini pieces into a large pot of salted boiling water set over high heat. Partially cover and let the water return to a boil. Cook for 3 minutes. Drain and let cool slightly.

8. In a very large bowl, combine the roasted eggplant, bell peppers, zucchini, onions, chopped tomatoes, tomato paste, 3 tablespoons of the remaining olive oil, and the salt and pepper; toss to combine. Make a *bouquet garni* by tying together the sprigs of oregano, thyme, and rosemary with string and add to the ratatouille, or simply stir in the dried herbs. Turn into the prepared casserole.

9. Bake, uncovered, for about 1½ hours, stirring once halfway through.

10. Remove from the oven and stir in the fresh basil and parsley. Let cool to room temperature. Stir in the remaining 2 tablespoons of olive oil. Cover and chill for several hours or several days. Remove the *bouquet garni* before serving.

Variations: This recipe is easily cut in half, or adjusted to your taste. You might want to use only 2 eggplants, or half the number of bell peppers. You can add even more peppers if desired. If you are using fresh herbs, consider adding 1 to 2 teaspoons of each, snipped, when adding the basil and parsley.

Reheat: This casserole is meant to be served cold.

Fragrant Fennel Casserole

A favorite for fall when fresh fennel bulbs come into the market, this casserole combines slices of the aniselike vegetable with a cream sauce and a crisp crumb topping. Since the flavor of fennel bulbs diminishes during cooking, I like to add crushed fennel seeds to boost their flavor. This casserole is fabulous reheated, so consider making it ahead.

MAKES: 6 to 8 servings

BAKES: At 375° F. for 30 to 40 minutes

CASSEROLE: Butter or oil a 13 × 9 × 2-inch casserole

6 medium (or 4 large) fennel bulbs, trimmed and cut lengthwise into ¼- to ½-inch slices (reserve the feathery leaves)

½ cup coarse fresh bread crumbs

4 tablespoons butter

1 onion, finely chopped

1 large garlic clove, minced or crushed through a press

½ teaspoon crushed fennel seeds

¼ teaspoon freshly grated nutmeg

⅛ teaspoon cayenne pepper (optional)

⅓ cup all-purpose flour

2½ cups milk

¼ cup dry sherry

¼ cup freshly grated Parmesan cheese

1 teaspoon salt

1. Adjust an oven shelf to the top third of the oven and preheat the oven. Prepare the casserole.

2. Bring a large pot of lightly salted water to a boil over high heat. Add the fennel bulbs, partially cover, and cook until tender when pierced with a fork, 5 to 8 minutes. Drain and reserve. Finely chop the feathery leaves and reserve.

3. Place the bread crumbs on a small baking sheet and bake until lightly toasted, about 5 minutes.

4. Melt the butter in a large saucepan over moderate heat. Add the onion and cook to soften, about 3 minutes. Add the garlic, fennel seeds, nutmeg, and cayenne pepper; cook 1 minute longer. Add the flour and stir with a fork to moisten. Cook 1 minute, stirring. Pour in the milk and stir until the sauce begins to thicken and simmer, about 3 minutes. Add the sherry, lower the heat, and simmer, stirring occasionally, for 3 to 5 minutes, until medium thick. Remove from the heat and stir in the Parmesan and salt.

5. Turn the fennel bulbs into the prepared casserole to make an even layer. Sprinkle with about ¼ cup of the chopped fennel leaves. Pour all of the sauce over the top and sprinkle with the toasted crumbs. Bake for 30 to 40 minutes, or until golden brown on top and bubbly around the edges. Let stand for 5 to 10 minutes before serving. Sprinkle with 2 to 3 tablespoons of the chopped fennel leaves and serve.

Variations: To make a meaty version, sauté 1 pound ground lean pork, chicken, or turkey with 1 minced garlic clove, ¼ teaspoon crushed fennel seeds, and ¼ teaspoon salt. Sprinkle with 2 tablespoons flour, then stir in ½ cup chicken stock or broth and ¼ cup dry sherry; stir over moderate heat until thickened and simmering. To assemble, arrange half the fennel bulbs in the casserole and top with all the meat filling, then half the sauce. Add the remaining fennel bulbs and remaining sauce, followed by the toasted crumbs.

Reheat: If at room temperature, bake uncovered at 350° F. for about 30 minutes. If cold, add 10 to 15 minutes.

Wild, Brown, and White Rice Pilaf

This big, rustic whole-grain casserole, fragrant with wild mushrooms and sesame oil, can be prepared hours in advance.

MAKES: 12 side-dish servings
BAKES: At 375° F. for 25 to 30 minutes
CASSEROLE: Butter or oil a 3½- to 4-quart or a 13 × 9 × 2-inch casserole

½ ounce dried porcini or cèpes

¾ cup hot water

1 cup wild rice, rinsed

6 cups light homemade chicken stock or canned broth

2 teaspoons salt

1½ cups long-grain brown rice

2 tablespoons unsalted butter

2 tablespoons olive oil

1 cup long-grain white rice

½ cup water

½ cup dry white wine

1 large onion, finely chopped

1 large garlic clove, minced or crushed through a press

½ teaspoon dried thyme, crumbled

8 ounces fresh mushrooms, thinly sliced

1 tablespoon Oriental sesame oil

1. Put the dried mushrooms in a small bowl and add the hot water. Set aside to soften for 30 to 60 minutes. Drain, reserving the soaking liquid. Finely chop the porcini.

2. Meanwhile, combine the wild rice, 2 cups of the chicken stock, and ½ teaspoon of the salt in a medium saucepan. Place over high heat and bring to a boil, stirring occasionally. Reduce the heat to low, cover tightly, and simmer gently until the grains are tender but not mushy, 30 to 60 minutes (this varies tremendously with the dryness of the wild rice). If the liquid has not been absorbed by the time the rice is tender, uncover and boil over high heat for a few minutes. Remove from the heat and reserve.

3. Put the brown rice in a nonstick large saucepan and place over moderately high heat. Toast, stirring frequently, for about 5 minutes, or until the grains begin to crackle and pop. Pour in 2 cups of the chicken stock. Strain the mushroom soaking liquid and add ½ cup. Stir in ½ teaspoon of the salt and 1 tablespoon of the butter, and bring to a boil. Reduce the heat to the lowest setting, cover, and simmer gently until the grains are tender but firm to the bite and the liquid is absorbed, about 35 minutes. Remove from the heat and let stand, covered, for 15 to 20 minutes.

4. Spoon 1 tablespoon of the olive oil into a heavy medium saucepan. Add the white rice and toast over moderate heat, stirring, until light golden brown, 4 to 5 minutes. Pour in the water and let it boil away. Stir in 1 cup of the chicken stock, the white wine, and ½ teaspoon salt, and bring to a boil over high heat. Reduce the heat to low, cover, and cook gently until tender but firm to the bite, 15 to 20 minutes. Remove from the heat. Remove the lid, cover with a double layer of paper towels, and replace the lid. Let stand for 15 minutes. Fluff with a fork.

5. Preheat the oven and prepare the casserole. Combine the remaining 1 tablespoon butter and 1 tablespoon olive oil in a large, heavy skillet over moderate heat. Add the onion and sauté to soften and lightly brown, 5 to 6 minutes. Add the garlic and thyme and cook for 1 to 2 minutes longer. Add the sliced mushrooms and the chopped porcini. Increase the heat and cook, tossing frequently, for about 3 minutes to soften and lightly brown. Add ½ cup of the chicken stock and the remaining ½ teaspoon salt and bring to a boil. Remove from the heat.

6. In a very large bowl, gently toss together the wild rice, brown rice, white rice, mushrooms, and sesame oil. Turn into the casserole or baking pan. Pour in the remaining ½ cup chicken stock and cover. Bake for 25 to 30 minutes, until the rice grains are tender. Serve hot.

Variations: Sauté 4 chopped carrots with the onion and add ½ cup chopped parsley when you combine the rices.

Reheat: If the casserole is at room temperature, reheat, covered, at 350°F. for 20 to 30 minutes. If cold, reheat at 350°F. for about 45 minutes, or until piping hot.

Brown Rice Casserole with Spinach Filling

Chock full of vegetables like zucchini, corn, carrots, and beans, this substantial vegetarian casserole will satisfy even the heartiest meat-eater.

MAKES: 8 servings
BAKES: At 350° F. for about 1 hour
CASSEROLE: Oil or butter a deep 3-quart casserole

1½ cups long-grain brown rice

1½ pounds fresh spinach, rinsed well and plucked of coarse stems, or 2 bags (10 ounces each) prewashed fresh spinach, or 1½ packages (10 ounces each) frozen spinach, thawed

½ large package (4 ounces) cream cheese, sliced

2 tablespoons fresh lemon juice

½ teaspoon dried tarragon (optional)

2½ teaspoons salt

2 tablespoons olive oil

2 onions, chopped

3 carrots, peeled and cut into ½-inch dice

1 cup fresh or frozen corn kernels

2 zucchini, trimmed and cut into ½-inch dice

2 to 3 large garlic cloves, minced or crushed through a press

2 teaspoons dried oregano, crumbled

2 teaspoons ground cumin

1 can (14 to 16 ounces) small red beans, black beans, pink beans, or pinto beans, drained, rinsed, and drained again

¼ teaspoon black pepper

4 large eggs

2 cups low-fat plain yogurt

¼ cup dry sherry or white wine or milk

¼ cup all-purpose flour

¾ cup freshly grated Parmesan cheese (3 ounces)

1. Bring 3 quarts of lightly salted water to a boil over high heat. Gradually add the rice, stirring so the boil does not stop. Partially cover the pan and boil until the rice is firm-tender, about 30 minutes. Drain in a colander, shaking a couple of times, until the dripping stops. Return the rice to the hot, dry pot, place a paper towel over the top, and cover with the lid. Let stand for at least 15 minutes (or prepare well in advance).

2. Place the spinach in a nonreactive large, heavy saucepan or dutch oven. Cover and cook over high heat until wilted down and cooked through, 3 to 5 minutes. Drain, pressing down on the spinach with a spoon to squeeze out some of the liquid. Coarsely chop the spinach and transfer it to a bowl. Stir in the cream cheese until melted. Add 1 tablespoon of the lemon juice, the tarragon, and ½ teaspoon of the salt; stir to blend. Reserve.

3. Preheat the oven, and prepare the casserole. Spoon the olive oil into a large, heavy skillet or sauté pan and place over moderate heat. Add the onions and carrots and sauté to soften slightly, 3 to 5 minutes. Add the corn, zucchini, garlic, oregano, cumin, and 1 teaspoon of the salt. Increase the heat to high and sauté to brown the vegetables, 7 to 10 minutes longer. Let cool slightly.

4. In a large bowl, toss together the rice, vegetable mixture, drained beans, the remaining 1 teaspoon salt, and the pepper.

5. In a bowl, whisk the eggs with the remaining 1 tablespoon lemon juice, the yogurt, and the sherry. Whisk in the flour and ½ cup of the Parmesan. Pour over the rice-vegetable mixture and fold together. Spoon half (about 5 cups) into the prepared casserole, making a level bottom layer. Spoon on the spinach filling and spread out evenly. Spoon on the remaining rice mixture; the casserole will be full. Sprinkle with the remaining ¼ cup Parmesan.

6. Bake in the center of the oven for about 1 hour, or until deep golden brown and bubbly around the edges. Let stand for at least 20 minutes before serving.

Variations: Add ⅓ cup chopped cilantro or slivered basil or 3 tablespoons snipped fresh dill to the rice mixture. To cut calories, use low-fat cream cheese.

Reheat: If at room temperature, bake, covered, at 350°F. for about 45 minutes. If cold, sprinkle with 2 to 3 tablespoons water, cover, and bake about 1¼ hours.

Almond Rice Pilaf

Dark Oriental sesame oil enhances the toasted nuttiness of almonds in a most delightful way. This side dish is so good that sometimes it's all I want for a main course!

MAKES: 4 to 6 side-dish servings
BAKES: At 350° F. for about 20 minutes
CASSEROLE: Butter or oil an 8-inch square or 1½- to 2-quart shallow casserole

4 teaspoons vegetable oil

½ cup slivered almonds (2 ounces)

1 onion, finely chopped

2 carrots, peeled and finely diced

1½ cups long-grain white rice

½ cup water

2 cups chicken stock or canned broth

½ teaspoon salt

¼ cup chopped fresh parsley

1 teaspoon unsalted butter

1 teaspoon Oriental sesame oil

1. Preheat the oven, and prepare the casserole.

2. Spoon 2 teaspoons of the vegetable oil into a heavy, medium saucepan over moderate heat. Add the almonds and toast, stirring frequently, until deep golden, 3 to 4 minutes. Turn out and reserve.

3. Spoon the remaining 2 teaspoons vegetable oil into the saucepan, add the onion and carrots, and sauté over moderate heat to soften, 3 to 5 minutes. Stir in the rice and cook, stirring frequently, until lightly toasted, 4 to 5 minutes.

4. Pour in the water and cook until it is absorbed, about 2 minutes. Add the chicken stock and salt. Bring to a boil. Remove from the heat and stir in the parsley, butter, sesame oil, and toasted almonds.

5. Turn into the prepared casserole; cover tightly. Bake for about 20 minutes, or until the rice is tender and the liquid is absorbed. Let stand, covered, for 10 minutes before serving. Uncover and fluff the grains. Serve hot.

Variations: Replace ¼ cup of the broth with white wine or sherry. Use cilantro or basil in place of the parsley and replace the sesame oil with 1 table-spoon olive oil.

Reheat: If the casserole is at room temperature, bake, covered, at 350°F. for 15 minutes. Uncover and fluff the grains. Cover and bake for 5 to 10 minutes longer, or until steaming hot; if cold, add 10 to 15 minutes before fluffing.

Two-Potato Casserole

Red-skinned boiling potatoes are layered like scalloped potatoes, but sandwiched with creamy mashed russet baking potatoes instead of milk or cream. The two varieties of potato have different textures and flavors that complement each other. Although I have used fresh sage leaves for flavoring, you can leave them out entirely for a simpler version.

MAKES: 8 to 10 side-dish servings
BAKES: At 375° F. for 1 to 1¼ hours
CASSEROLE: Generously butter a deep 3-quart casserole

3 pounds russet baking potatoes (6 large)

2 large garlic cloves, sliced

Salt

½ large package (4 ounces) cream cheese, cut up

2 tablespoons unsalted butter

⅓ cup milk

⅓ cup light cream or half-and-half

¼ teaspoon black pepper

¼ teaspoon freshly grated nutmeg

½ cup finely chopped red bell pepper (optional)

1 tablespoon cider vinegar

2 pounds red-skinned potatoes (6 medium)

25 fresh medium sage leaves, halved

1. Preheat the oven, and prepare the casserole.

2. Peel the russet potatoes, cut them into 1-inch chunks, and drop them into a large pot of cold water. Add the garlic and a pinch of salt. Partially cover the pot and boil over moderately high heat until the potatoes are tender when pierced with a fork, 15 to 20 minutes. Drain and return the potatoes to the pot.

3. Shake the pot over moderate heat for 30 seconds to dry. Add the cream cheese, butter, milk, light cream, 1½ teaspoons salt, the pepper, and nutmeg. Beat with an electric mixer or mash with a potato masher until fluffy. Stir in the bell pepper and cider vinegar.

4. Remove and reserve 1 cup of the mashed potatoes for the top. Peel the red-skinned potatoes and hold them in a bowl of cold water. Remove 1 potato at a time and cut it lengthwise in half. Cut crosswise into ¼-inch slices and arrange in the prepared casserole. Spoon on 1 cup of the mashed potatoes in dabs and spread carefully so as not to disturb the sliced potatoes. Add 10 sage leaf halves. Repeat the layering 5 more times, spreading the reserved cup of mashed potatoes over the top.

5. Cover the casserole and bake for 1 to 1¼ hours, or until lightly browned on top and the potatoes are tender when pierced with a long skewer or fork. Remove from the oven and let stand for 15 to 20 minutes before serving.

Variations: Instead of fresh sage leaves, add about ¼ cup chopped fresh basil or 3 tablespoons snipped fresh oregano or thyme (or a combination), or 1 tablespoon snipped fresh rosemary. Crumbled bacon or minced ham can be added to the layers for a smoky flavor.

Reheat: If at room temperature, cover and reheat at 350°F. for for about 45 minutes; if cold, add about 15 minutes.

Potato-Gorgonzola Casserole

This satisfying cheese-and-potato casserole is rich and pungent from the creamy gorgonzola cheese. I recommend searching for the Bel Gioioso brand of gorgonzola, made by Auricchio in Wisconsin. It closely resembles the gorgonzola dolce of Italy, rather than the more-aged crumbly kind. Serve this with roasted beef, chicken, or pork or with big grilled beef burgers on toasted rolls and slices of juicy summer tomatoes.

MAKES: 4 to 6 servings
BAKES: At 400° F. for about 30 minutes
CASSEROLE: Oil a shallow 2-quart casserole

2 pounds red-skinned potatoes (8 medium), boiled until tender and cooled

6 tablespoons light cream or half-and-half

4 tablespoons chopped fresh parsley

¾ teaspoon salt

Black pepper

8 ounces soft, creamy gorgonzola cheese, such as Bel Gioioso

¼ cup freshly grated Parmesan cheese

1. Adjust an oven shelf to the top third of the oven and preheat the oven. Prepare the casserole.

2. Peel the potatoes and cut them lengthwise in half, and then crosswise into ¼-inch half-rounds. Layer one-third of the slices in the prepared casserole.

3. Drizzle 2 tablespoons of the light cream over the potatoes; sprinkle with 2 tablespoons of the parsley, ¼ teaspoon of the salt, and a few grinds of pepper. Cut half of the gorgonzola into bits and scatter over the top. Repeat the layering once more, and then top that layer with the remaining one-third potato slices, ¼ teaspoon salt, pepper, and 2 tablespoons cream. Sprinkle the Parmesan over the top.

4. Bake in the top third of the oven for about 30 minutes, or until bubbly and lightly browned. Let stand for 15 minutes before serving.

Variations: Use another creamy blue cheese, such as Saga Blue instead of gorgonzola. Use Yukon Gold or Yellow Finn potatoes instead of red-skinned.

Reheat: If at room temperature, bake, uncovered, at 350°F. for about 30 minutes. If cold, add 10 to 15 minutes.

Tangy Cheddar Potato Casserole

This comforting casserole has a creamy consistency with the tangy bite of sour cream and yogurt. It tastes great with most outdoor barbecues and is a welcome addition to any Sunday supper. It is simple to put together, but just remember to boil the potatoes a day ahead so they can chill and firm up before grating.

MAKES: 4 to 6 side-dish servings
BAKES: At 350°F. for 50 to 60 minutes
CASSEROLE: Butter or oil an 8-inch square shallow 2-quart casserole

1½ pounds red-skinned potatoes (6 medium), scrubbed

1 cup sour cream

1 cup low-fat plain yogurt

¼ cup milk

1 onion, grated

2 tablespoons all-purpose flour

1 teaspoon salt

¼ teaspoon black pepper

¼ teaspoon cayenne pepper

1½ cups grated sharp cheddar cheese (6 ounces)

¼ cup freshly grated Parmesan cheese (1 ounce)

½ teaspoon sweet paprika

1. A day ahead, put the potatoes in a large, heavy pot and add cold water to cover generously. Add a big pinch of salt. Place over moderately high heat, partially cover, and bring to a boil. Boil until tender when pierced with a long fork, 30 to 40 minutes. Drain and let cool to room temperature. Chill for at least 4 hours or overnight.

2. Adjust an oven shelf to the upper third of the oven and preheat the oven. Prepare the casserole.

3. In a large bowl, stir together the sour cream, yogurt, and milk. Stir in the grated onion, flour, salt, pepper, and cayenne.

4. Peel the potatoes and coarsely grate them through the largest holes of a cheese grater. Add to the bowl, along with the cheddar, and stir gently to combine. Turn the mixture into the prepared casserole. Sprinkle with the Parmesan and paprika (it looks nice when sprinkled in diagonal lines).

5. Bake for 50 to 60 minutes, or until golden brown on top and bubbly around the edges. Cool in the pan on a rack for 20 minutes before serving.

Variations: Swiss Emmentaler cheese can be used in place of the cheddar. For a smoky flavor, use smoked Gouda. For a sharper flavor, use sharp provolone. One-half cup sliced scallions can be added instead of the grated onion and 2 to 3 tablespoons of chopped fresh herbs, such as oregano or basil, can be added with the potatoes.

Reheat: If at room temperature, heat at 350°F. for about 30 minutes. A cold casserole will take about 1 hour.

| Potato-Cheddar Kugel |

Kugels are wonderful Jewish casseroles. This one is a savory potato-and-cheese casserole that you can reheat over and over again and it just gets better and better. I like it a lot.

MAKES: 6 side-dish servings
BAKES: At 350°F. for 1 hour and at 400°F. for 15 minutes
CASSEROLE: Butter or oil a shallow 2-quart casserole

2 pounds red-skinned boiling potatoes (8 medium)

4 large eggs

1 cup low-fat plain yogurt

½ cup light cream, half-and-half, or milk

¼ cup all-purpose flour

1½ teaspoons baking powder

1 teaspoon salt

¼ teaspoon freshly grated nutmeg

⅛ teaspoon black pepper

2 onions

1 cup grated sharp cheddar cheese (4 ounces)

1½ tablespoons melted butter or olive oil

1. Preheat the oven, and prepare the casserole.

2. Peel the potatoes and coarsely grate them through the largest holes of a cheese grater into a large bowl of cold water. Let soak until needed.

3. In a large bowl, whisk the eggs to blend. Whisk in the yogurt and light cream.

4. In a small bowl, stir together the flour, baking powder, salt, nutmeg, and pepper.

5. Drain the potatoes in a colander. Remove by small handfuls, squeezing out the excess water, and stir into the egg mixture along with the flour mixture. Cut the stem ends off the onions (do not cut off the root ends) and peel them. Coarsely grate the onions over the potato mixture. Stir in the cheese and melted butter. Discard root ends.

6. Turn into the casserole. Bake for 1 hour.

7. Increase the oven temperature to 400°F. and bake for about 15 minutes longer, until deep golden brown. Let stand for at least 15 minutes before serving.

Variations: Substitute Swiss cheese, smoked gouda, or freshly grated Parmesan for the cheddar.

Reheat: If the casserole is cold, cover with aluminum foil and bake at 325°F. for 45 to 60 minutes or until steam escapes when uncovered. Increase the oven temperature to 425°F., uncover, and bake for about 10 minutes longer.

Roasted Red Pepper and Potato Casserole

The big flavors of roasted red peppers, fresh basil, and provolone cheese permeate a creamy sauce that naps slices of russet potatoes.

MAKES: 6 to 8 servings

BAKES: At 375°F. for 30 to 40 minutes

CASSEROLE: Butter or oil a 13 × 9 × 2-inch casserole

1 pound red bell peppers (3 to 4 medium)

4 tablespoons unsalted butter

1 pound fresh mushrooms, cut into ¼-inch slices

2½ pounds russet baking potatoes (8 to 9 medium), peeled and held in cold water

¼ cup plus 2 tablespoons all-purpose flour

2 cups milk

1 cup strong chicken stock or condensed canned broth

¼ cup dry white wine or vermouth

1 teaspoon salt

⅛ teaspoon black pepper

1 cup grated sharp provolone cheese (4 ounces)

¾ cup lightly packed slivered fresh basil leaves

½ teaspoon sweet paprika

1. Roast the peppers by placing them directly in the flame of a gas burner or about 3 inches below an electric broiler. Turn them frequently until they are blistered and charred all over. Let cool for 1 or 2 minutes, then place in a plastic bag, twisting to enclose. Let cool to room temperature. Rub off the charred skins with your fingers, or work over a colander under gently running water to rub the skins away. Slit open the peppers and remove the seeds, ribs, and stems. Cut the peppers into 1-inch squares.

2. Preheat the oven, and prepare the casserole.

3. Preheat a large, heavy skillet over moderate heat. Add 1 tablespoon of the butter and swirl to melt. Add all of the mushrooms and press them into an even layer but do not toss. Increase the heat to high and brown well, about 3 minutes. Toss and cook until cooked through and the juices have boiled away, 3 to 4 minutes longer. Turn into a bowl and reserve.

4. Bring a large pot of lightly salted water to a boil over high heat. Meanwhile, cut the potatoes into ¼-inch slices and place them in cold water. Drain well and drop the slices into the boiling water. Cover and boil until tender but firm to the bite, 5 to 7 minutes. Drain and reserve.

5. Melt the remaining 3 tablespoons butter in a heavy, medium saucepan set over moderate heat. When melted, stir in the flour and cook, stirring, for about 2 minutes. The mixture will be dry, but it is best to use minimal butter. Stirring constantly, pour in the milk and chicken stock. Stir with a fork or whisk over moderate heat until the sauce just begins to thicken but is not yet simmering. Stir in the wine, salt, and pepper. Reduce the heat to low and simmer, stirring frequently, for 2 to 3 minutes to make a medium-thick sauce. Remove from the heat and stir in ¾ cup of the cheese and the basil.

6. Layer half of the potato slices in the casserole. Arrange half of the mushrooms and half of the peppers on top. Spoon on half of the basil-provolone sauce. Repeat with the remaining ingredients. Sprinkle the top with the remaining ¼ cup provolone and the paprika.

7. Bake in the top third of the oven for 30 to 40 minutes, or until bubbly and golden brown. Let stand for 10 minutes or longer before serving. (If making more than 6 hours in advance, cover with aluminum foil and refrigerate or freeze.)

Variations: Substitute Parmesan or Jarlsberg cheese for the provolone. One-half cup chopped fresh parsley can be substituted for the fresh basil. Substitute cheddar for the provolone and cilantro for the basil.

Reheat: If at room temperature, bake at 350°F. for about 20 minutes; if cold, add about 15 minutes.

Spinach, Mushroom, and Potato Oven Omelet

Ideal for brunch or supper, this baked omelet casserole can be kept hot in its water bath for at least an hour after baking. A good browning of the potatoes adds a deep flavor dimension enhanced with fresh basil. I like to serve sliced tomatoes alongside.

MAKES: 4 to 6 servings

BAKES: At 325° F. for 1 to 1¼ hours

CASSEROLE: Butter or oil an 8- or 9-inch square casserole

1 pound fresh spinach, or 1 cup cooked chopped spinach

1 pound red-skinned potatoes (4 to 6 small)

1½ tablespoons olive oil

1½ teaspoons salt

1 onion, finely chopped

8 ounces fresh mushrooms, thinly sliced

1 tablespoon unsalted butter

½ cup lightly packed fresh basil leaves

8 large eggs

½ cup half-and-half

½ cup plain yogurt

1 tablespoon all-purpose flour

¼ teaspoon black pepper

¼ teaspoon freshly grated nutmeg

1 cup coarsely shredded sharp cheddar cheese (4 ounces)

1. Preheat the oven, and prepare the casserole. Choose a large roasting pan to act as a hot water bath.

2. Rinse the spinach thoroughly and pull off any thick or tough stems. Put the wet spinach into a nonreactive large pot, cover, and cook over high heat, stirring once or twice, until wilted and cooked down, 3 to 4 minutes. Drain and let cool; chop.

3. Peel the potatoes and cut them into ¼-inch slices. Spoon the olive oil into a large, heavy skillet and place over moderately high heat. Add the potatoes and sprinkle with ½ teaspoon of the salt. Brown well, tossing occasionally, until light golden brown, about 5 minutes. Add the onion and cook until deep golden brown and tender, about 10 minutes. Turn out onto a platter and reserve.

4. Add the mushrooms and butter to the skillet and sauté to lightly brown, about 3 minutes. Turn out over the potatoes.

5. In a food processor or blender, combine the spinach, basil, 2 of the eggs, and the half-and-half. Blend to a puree.

6. In a large bowl, whisk the remaining 6 eggs. Add the pureed spinach mixture, the yogurt, flour, pepper, nutmeg, and the remaining 1 teaspoon salt. Whisk to blend. Stir in the mushrooms, potatoes, and cheddar. Turn into the casserole.

7. Place the casserole into the larger pan, and add hot tap water to reach halfway up the sides. Bake 1 to 1¼ hours, or until set and the tip of a knife comes out clean when inserted in the center. Serve right away or keep hot in the hot water bath. If desired, leave in the turned-off oven for 1 to 2 hours. Serve hot, warm, or cold.

Variations: Replace the spinach with chopped cooked Swiss chard and the basil with cilantro; add ½ cup sliced scallions and a clove of garlic, if desired. Poblanos or jalapeño chilies may be added as well.

Reheat: If at room temperature, reheat at 325°F. for about 30 minutes; if cold, heat at 350°F. for 45 to 60 minutes.

Mashed Potato–Broccoli Casserole

Although I created this as a side dish to accompany roast chicken and meats or charcoal-grilled steaks and prime ribs of beef, it also makes a great vegetarian main course for supper or lunch.

MAKES: 4 to 6 servings
BAKES: At 325°F. for 35 to 40 minutes
CASSEROLE: Butter a shallow 8- or 9-inch square casserole

4 cups packed broccoli florets

2 pounds russet baking potatoes (4 large)

½ cup light cream or milk

2 tablespoons unsalted butter

⅛ teaspoon black pepper

¼ teaspoon freshly grated nutmeg

⅛ teaspoon cayenne pepper

1 teaspoon salt

1 large egg

2 tablespoons dry white wine

1 cup diced (¼ inch) sharp cheddar cheese (4 ounces) and ¼ cup grated sharp cheddar cheese (1 ounce)

½ teaspoon sweet paprika

1. Preheat the oven, and prepare the casserole.

2. Drop the broccoli florets into a large pot of lightly salted boiling water over high heat. Cover and blanch until crisp-tender, 2 to 3 minutes after the boil returns. Drain and reserve.

3. Peel the potatoes and cut them into 1-inch chunks, dropping them into a large pot of cold water as they are cut. Add a big pinch of salt and bring to a boil over high heat. Partially cover the pan and boil over moderately high heat until tender when pierced with a fork, 15 to 20 minutes.

4. Drain the potatoes and return them to the dry pot. Shake over moderate heat for 30 seconds to dry. Add the cream and bring it to a boil; turn off the heat. Add the butter, salt, black pepper, nutmeg, and cayenne. Beat with a hand-held electric mixer or mash with a potato masher until fluffy. Add the egg and wine and beat until blended. Stir in the broccoli and cubed cheddar.

5. Turn into the prepared pan and make a few swirls on top. Sprinkle with the grated cheddar and the paprika. Bake for 35 to 40 minutes, or until golden brown. Let stand for 10 minutes. Serve hot.

Variations: Instead of the cheddar, try adding Gruyère, provolone, or smoked Gouda cheese. Use Cognac or brandy in place of the white wine.

Reheat: If at room temperature, cover with aluminum foil and reheat at 350°F. for about 20 minutes. Uncover and bake until heated through, about 10 minutes longer; if cold, add about 15 minutes before uncovering.

Potato-Porcini Casserole

Here's an earthy casserole that's at home for brunch or supper and perfect for a picnic. One thing I like about an egg-and-potato casserole like this is that there's no last-minute fuss. Just ½ ounce of dried porcini contributes fabulous fall forest flavor year-round. The Spanish potato omelet called a *tortilla* was the inspiration for this oven-baked version. It is good hot, warm, cool, or cold.

MAKES: 6 servings
BAKES: At 300° F. for about 1 hour
CASSEROLE: Lightly oil an 8- or 9-inch square casserole

½ **ounce dried porcini, cèpes, or other black European mushrooms**

½ **cup hot water**

2 **pounds red-skinned or waxy boiling potatoes (8 medium), peeled, cut into ½-inch dice, and held in cold water**

1 **tablespoon unsalted butter**

1 **pound large fresh mushrooms, cut into ½-inch dice**

½ **cup sliced whole scallions**

¼ **cup chopped fresh parsley (optional)**

6 **large eggs**

¾ **cup freshly grated Parmesan or romano cheese (3 ounces)**

2 **tablespoons all-purpose flour**

½ **large package (4 ounces) cream cheese, softened**

¼ **cup milk or light cream**

¼ **cup dry white wine**

1 **teaspoon dried basil, crumbled**

1 **teaspoon salt, or a pinch more**

⅛ **teaspoon black pepper, or a pinch more**

½ **teaspoon sweet paprika**

1. Put the porcini in a cup and pour in the hot water; set aside to soften for 30 to 60 minutes. Remove the porcini with a slotted spoon and lightly squeeze out any excess liquid. Chop the mushrooms and reserve. Sometimes sand is present in dried mushrooms; gently pour ¼ cup of the soaking liquid into a cup, leaving any grit behind.

2. Bring a large pot of lightly salted water to a boil over high heat. Drain the diced potatoes and add to the water; cook until firm-tender, 5 to 7 minutes from the time they hit the water. Drain and reserve.

3. Preheat the oven, and prepare the casserole.

4. Preheat a large, heavy skillet over moderate heat. Add the butter, swirling the pan to coat. Add the fresh mushrooms, increase the heat to high, and let brown without stirring, 2 to 3 minutes. Toss and cook until the liquid boils away, 3 to 4 minutes longer.

5. In a large bowl, toss together the potatoes, sautéed mushrooms, scallions, and parsley.

6. In a blender or food processor, combine the eggs with the chopped porcini and the ¼ cup soaking liquid. Add all but 2 tablespoons of the Parmesan, along with the flour, cream cheese, milk, wine, basil, salt, and pepper; process until pureed. Pour over the potato mushroom mixture and toss.

7. Turn the mixture into the prepared pan; sprinkle with the reserved 2 tablespoons Parmesan and the paprika. Bake for about 1 hour, or until the center is set (a knife tip inserted in the center will come out clean). Let stand for at least 15 minutes, or cool until warm, or at room temperature. Cut into rectangles and serve.

Variations: Instead of using porcini, substitute 1 ounce (½ cup) sun-dried tomatoes: Soak in boiling water for 3 to 5 minutes to soften, and then chop. Reserve ¼ cup of the soaking liquid and proceed with the recipe. When using sun-dried tomatoes, try substituting fresh basil for the parsley.

Reheat: If the casserole is at room temperature, reheat at 325°F. for about 30 minutes. If cold, reheat at 350°F. for about 45 minutes.

Bow Tie Four-Cheese Casserole

This is an elevated version of macaroni and cheese, flavored with four cheeses, none of which is cheddar or American. Italian bow tie pasta (*farfalle*) is made of hard durum wheat, and retains its good texture even after being baked, cooled, and reheated the next day. You might think this makes a big quantity of sauce for just 8 ounces of pasta, but much of the liquid is absorbed and the sauce cooks down a little during baking. The end result, however, is pasta bow ties in a wonderfully creamy sauce that has a big cheese flavor.

MAKES: 6 servings
BAKES: At 375° F. for about 30 minutes
CASSEROLE: Butter a 2½- to 3-quart casserole

Salt

8 ounces imported bow tie pasta (*farfalle*)

2 tablespoons olive oil

2 tablespoons unsalted butter

½ cup all-purpose flour

4 cups milk

¼ teaspoon freshly grated nutmeg

1 teaspoon salt

⅛ to ¼ teaspoon cayenne pepper

¼ cup dry white wine

1 cup crumbled gorgonzola or other crumbly blue cheese (4 ounces)

1 cup Monterey Jack cheese, grated (4 ounces)

½ large package (4 ounces) cream cheese, cut up

½ cup Parmesan cheese, grated (2 ounces)

¼ cup chopped fresh parsley (optional)

1. Preheat the oven, and prepare the casserole.

2. Bring a large pot of water to a boil over high heat. Add about 1 tablespoon salt. When the water is at a full boil, drop in the pasta and stir constantly with a slotted spoon until the boil returns. Cook, stirring occasionally, until tender but slightly firm, 12 to 14 minutes. Drain in a colander, shaking well.

3. Meanwhile, combine the olive oil and butter in a nonreactive heavy, medium saucepan over moderate heat. When the butter melts, add the flour and stir to moisten. Cook, stirring frequently, for 1 to 2 minutes. The mixture will be dry. Pour in all of the milk and add 1 teaspoon salt, the nutmeg, and cayenne (using the larger amount if you want to taste some heat or the lesser amount for just a spark of flavor). Stirring constantly, bring to a simmer and cook until thick and smooth, 2 to 3 minutes.

4. Stir the wine into the sauce and simmer, stirring, for 2 to 3 minutes longer. Remove from the heat and stir in the gorgonzola, Monterey Jack, cream cheese, and all but 2 tablespoons of the Parmesan. Add the drained pasta and the parsley; toss to thoroughly coat the pasta with sauce.

5. Turn the mixture into the prepared casserole; sprinkle with the reserved Parmesan. Bake in the center of the oven for about 30 minutes, or until golden brown and bubbly. Remove from the oven and let stand for at least 30 minutes before serving. Or, let cool to room temperature, and then cover and chill.

Variations: You can add about 1 cup of small pieces of sliced smoked ham and/or 1 cup of baby green peas when you toss in the pasta. Also, try adding about ½ pound sliced fresh mushrooms, which you have first lightly browned in butter.

Reheat: If at room temperature, cover and bake at 350°F. for about 30 minutes; if cold, add about 15 minutes.

Tortellini in Creamy Roquefort Sauce

This rich and wonderful casserole shows off the complex tortellini textures, all those folds and pleats making crevices to trap the creamy Roquefort sauce. It is dotted with green peas and roasted red peppers.

MAKES: 6 to 8 servings
BAKES: At 425° F. for 17 to 20 minutes
CASSEROLE: Butter a shallow 12 × 8-inch casserole

1 package (10 ounces) frozen green peas

1 pound fresh or frozen cheese tortellini

3 tablespoons unsalted butter

1 small garlic clove, minced

¼ cup all-purpose flour

2½ cups milk

¼ cup heavy cream or milk

¼ cup dry white wine

¼ teaspoon freshly grated nutmeg

½ teaspoon salt

⅛ teaspoon black pepper

1 cup crumbled Roquefort cheese (4 ounces)

1 red bell pepper, roasted, peeled, trimmed (see page 58), and cut into ½-inch squares

¼ cup grated Parmesan cheese (1 ounce)

1. Adjust a shelf to the top third of the oven and preheat the oven; prepare the casserole.

2. In a medium saucepan, bring 1 cup of water to a boil over high heat. Add the peas and blanch for 1 minute after the boil returns. Drain and reserve.

3. Bring a large pot of lightly salted water to a boil over high heat. Drop in the tortellini, partially cover, and cook, stirring occasionally, until the water returns to a boil. Lower the heat slightly and boil gently, stirring occasionally, until tender but firm to the bite, 8 to 10 minutes for frozen tortellini, 5 to 6 minutes for fresh. Drain in a colander.

4. Meanwhile, make the sauce so it is ready when the pasta is drained. Melt the butter in a large saucepan over moderate heat. Add the garlic and cook for 15 seconds. Stir in the flour and cook, stirring, for 1 to 2 minutes; the mixture will be dry. Stir in 1 cup of the milk until smooth. Add the remaining 1½ cups milk and the cream. Stir or whisk constantly until the sauce thickens and comes to a simmer. Add the wine, nutmeg, salt, and pepper, and stir until thick. Simmer over low heat, stirring occasionally, for about 5 minutes.

5. Remove the sauce from the heat and stir in the Roquefort. Fold in the bell pepper and peas. Add the drained tortellini, and toss to combine.

6. Turn the mixture into the prepared casserole and sprinkle with the Parmesan. Bake in the top third of the hot oven for 17 to 20 minutes, or until golden brown and bubbly. Let stand for 5 minutes. Serve hot.

Variations: Add a smoky accent by tossing in ½ cup chopped smoked ham along with the peas and bell peppers.

Reheat: Sprinkle with 1 tablespoon of water, cover with aluminum foil, and bake in the top third of a 350°F. oven for 30 minutes. Uncover, increase the oven temperature to 425°F., and bake for 10 to 15 minutes longer to crisp the top slightly. If the casserole is cold, bake for 35 to 40 minutes before increasing the heat.

| Wisconsin Lasagne |

Thin, luscious, and saucy, this cheese lasagne was inspired by a trip to big cheese country: Wisconsin. Quite simple to put together, all you do is cook lasagna noodles and make a cheese sauce. Although you can substitute Parmesan or romano for the Pepato, I encourage you to look for Pepato, a rich peppercorn-studded romano type of cheese. The flavors blossom to their fullest when the lasagne is cooled to room temperature and then reheated.

MAKES: 8 servings
BAKES: At 350° F. for 30 to 35 minutes
CASSEROLE: Butter or oil a 13 × 9 × 2-inch casserole

9 curly-edged lasagna noodles (about 8 ounces)

3 tablespoons unsalted butter

1 large garlic clove, minced

¼ cup all-purpose flour

4 cups milk

1 teaspoon salt

¼ teaspoon black or white pepper

¼ teaspoon freshly grated nutmeg

⅛ teaspoon cayenne pepper (optional)

1½ cups grated mild provolone cheese (6 ounces)

1½ cups grated Pepato cheese (6 ounces)

½ large package (4 ounces) cream cheese, sliced

½ teaspoon sweet paprika

1. Preheat the oven, and prepare the casserole. Bring a large, wide pot of salted water to a boil over high heat.

2. Place the lasagna noodles in the boiling water and stir gently until the boil resumes. Partially cover and boil under tender but firm to the bite, 10 to 12 minutes. Drain. Hold the lasagna noodles in a large bowl of cold water for up to 10 minutes.

3. Meanwhile, combine the butter and garlic in a medium saucepan over moderate heat. Let the butter melt and the garlic sizzle gently without coloring, about 1 minutes. Add the flour and cook, stirring, for 1 to 2 minutes. Pour in half of the milk. Whisk constantly over moderate heat until thickened and at a simmer. Add the remaining 2 cups of milk, the salt, pepper, nutmeg, and cayenne; stir frequently until the simmer returns. Reduce the heat and simmer, stirring frequently, for 5 minutes.

4. Remove the sauce from the heat. Combine the provolone and Pepato cheeses; reserve ½ cup of the mixture and add the remainder to the sauce along with the cream cheese. Stir the sauce until smooth and the cheeses are melted.

5. Drain the noodles and spread them out in a single layer on a towel or paper towels. Arrange 3 lasagna noodles in the prepared casserole (it doesn't matter if they do not quite touch because they will swell slightly upon baking). Ladle on about one-third of the sauce. Repeat the layering 2 more times. Sprinkle the top with the reserved ½ cup mixed cheeses and the paprika.

6. Bake for 30 to 35 minutes, or until golden brown on top and bubbly around the edges. Let stand for about 15 minutes before cutting into squares and serving.

Variations: Substitute Parmesan or romano for the Pepato and a little cracked pepper. Bel Paese or low-fat cream cheese can be used instead of cream cheese. For a sensational cheese and mushroom lasagne, sauté 1 pound of sliced fresh mushrooms in a skillet with 1½ tablespoons butter over moderately high heat until lightly browned; pour in ½ cup dry white wine and toss until completely evaporated, 4 to 5 minutes longer. When assembling, add half the mushrooms to each of the first 2 layers.

Reheat: Cover with aluminum foil. If at room temperature, reheat at 350°F. for about 30 minutes; if cold, add about 15 minutes.

Artichoke Lasagne with Tomato-Basil Sauce

This is hearty vegetarian fare at its best. Since the lasagne is excellent when reheated, I suggest you make it ahead. By the way, most of the tomato-basil sauce is spooned over the lasagne after it has baked; very little goes into the layering.

MAKES: 8 servings

BAKES: At 350° F. for about 45 minutes

CASSEROLE: Generously butter or oil a 13 × 9 × 2-inch casserole or lasagne pan

1 recipe Tomato-Basil Sauce (recipe follows)

4 large, firm, tightly closed artichokes (12 to 16 ounces each)

3 tablespoons fresh lemon juice

2 tablespoons olive oil

3 tablespoons unsalted butter

½ cup dry white wine

½ cup water

1½ teaspoons salt

2 pounds whole or part-skim ricotta cheese

1 pound whole or part-skim mozzarella cheese, coarsely shredded (4 cups)

1 cup freshly grated Parmesan cheese (4 ounces)

1 large egg

½ cup milk

½ cup chopped fresh parsley

1½ teaspoons dried oregano, crumbled

¼ teaspoon freshly grated nutmeg

¼ teaspoon black pepper

15 curly-edged lasagna noodles (12 to 14 ounces)

8 small fresh basil sprigs, for serving (optional)

1. Prepare the Tomato-Basil Sauce in advance.

2. Cut off all but 1 inch from the artichoke stems. Snap off the outer leaves, working all around, until you reach the tightly closed bud of pale green leaves. Rub with a cut lemon to prevent darkening. Trim off any tough outer layer with a paring knife. Quarter the artichokes lengthwise and scrape out the fuzzy chokes. Cut each quarter into 4 equal wedges and drop into a bowl of water and 2 tablespoons of the lemon juice.

3. In a nonreactive large saucepan, combine 1 tablespoon of the olive oil and 1 tablespoon of the butter, and place over moderate heat. Pour in the wine and water. Add the remaining 1 tablespoon lemon juice and ½ teaspoon of the salt. Bring to a boil. Drain the artichoke wedges and add them. Partially cover and cook until almost tender, about 10 minutes. Uncover, increase the heat, and boil until the liquid evaporates and the artichokes begin to sizzle. Continue cooking until lightly browned, 3 to 5 minutes longer. Remove from the heat and set aside to cool.

4. In a large bowl, stir together the ricotta cheese, 3 cups of the mozzarella, and ½ cup of the Parmesan. Beat in the egg, milk, 1 tablespoon of the butter, parsley, oregano, nutmeg, pepper, and remaining 1 teaspoon salt.

5. Preheat the oven and prepare the casserole or lasagne pan.

6. Bring a large, wide pot of lightly salted water to a boil over high heat. Add the noodles, one at a time, placing them in different directions. Stir gently with a slotted spoon–to keep them moving so they do not stick together–until the boil returns. Cook until tender but firm to the bite, 10 to 12 minutes. The noodles will cook further as they bake. Drain and rinse in a bowl of cold water. Lay out flat in a single layer on a towel or paper towels.

7. Spread ½ cup of the Tomato-Basil Sauce over the bottom of the pan. Arrange 5 of the noodles slightly overlapping in the pan to cover, trimming if needed to fit. Spoon in half of the ricotta filling, and arrange half of the artichokes over the filling. Spoon on another ½ cup of Tomato-Basil Sauce, and repeat the layering with 5 more noodles, the remaining filling and artichokes, and ½ cup Tomato-Basil Sauce. Top with the remaining 5 noodles, trimmed to fit as before. Spread the noodles with ½ cup of the Tomato-Basil Sauce, and drizzle with the remaining 1 tablespoon olive oil. Dot with the remaining 1 tablespoon butter. Scatter the remaining 1 cup of mozzarella and ¼ cup of the remaining Parmesan over the top.

8. Coat the dull side of a large sheet of aluminum foil with olive oil, and invert it over the lasagne. Cover tightly and bake for 45 minutes. Loosen the foil and let stand for 15 to 20 minutes before serving.

9. Heat the remaining 3½ cups of Tomato-Basil Sauce. Cut the lasagne into squares and serve hot with the sauce and the remaining ¼ cup Parmesan. Garnish each serving with a basil sprig, if desired.

Variation: Substitute two 10-ounce packages frozen artichoke hearts for the fresh and cut them into wedges and jump to step 3.

Reheat: Sprinkle 2 tablespoons water over the lasagne and cover with aluminum foil. If at room temperature, bake for about 40 minutes; if cold, add about 15 minutes.

| Tomato-Basil Sauce |

MAKES: About 5 cups

2 tablespoons olive oil

1 carrot, peeled and finely chopped

1 onion, finely chopped

2 large garlic cloves, minced or crushed through a press

½ teaspoon dried oregano, crumbled

½ teaspoon dried thyme, crumbled

1 bay leaf

1 can (28 ounces) crushed tomatoes

1 cup water

1 cup dry white wine

2 tablespoons tomato paste

1 teaspoon salt

¼ teaspoon black pepper

½ cup chopped fresh basil leaves

1 teaspoon unsalted butter

½ teaspoon sugar (optional)

1. Spoon the olive oil into a nonreactive medium saucepan and place over moderate heat. Add the carrot and onion and sauté until softened, 3 to 5 minutes. Add the garlic, oregano, thyme, and bay leaf and cook for 1 to 2 minutes longer.

2. Add the crushed tomatoes, water, wine, tomato paste, salt, and pepper. Bring to a boil. Reduce the heat to low and simmer until the sauce is thick, rich, and reduced to 5 cups, about 30 minutes. Remove from the heat and stir in the basil, butter, and sugar. (If making ahead, cool to room temperature. Cover and refrigerate for up to a week.)

Brewsky Cheese Grits

Both beer and chicken broth boost the flavor of cheese grits, and garlic and Worcestershire sauce are added for sensation. Serve this robust, home-style casserole of Southern inspiration for breakfast, brunch, lunch, or supper.

MAKES: 6 side-dish servings
BAKES: At 350° F. for 20 to 25 minutes
CASSEROLE: Butter or oil a 12 × 8-inch shallow casserole

2 cups chicken stock or canned broth

½ cup beer or ale

1 large garlic clove, minced or crushed through a press

¼ teaspoon salt

½ cup old-fashioned (not quick-cooking) grits

1¼ cups shredded sharp cheddar cheese (6 ounces)

½ cup freshly grated Parmesan cheese (2 ounces)

3 large eggs

2 teaspoons Worcestershire sauce

⅛ teaspoon cayenne pepper (optional)

⅛ teaspoon black pepper

½ teaspoon sweet paprika

1. Preheat the oven, and prepare the casserole.

2. In a nonstick medium saucepan, combine the chicken stock, beer, garlic, and salt; bring to a boil over high heat. Lower the heat and gradually stir in the grits. Bring the mixture back to a boil, stirring constantly. Cover and cook over low heat, stirring frequently, until tender and very thick, about 20 minutes.

3. Remove the pan from the heat and stir in 1 cup of the cheddar and ⅓ cup of the Parmesan.

4. In a large bowl, whisk the eggs to blend. Whisk in the Worcestershire sauce, cayenne, and black pepper. Gradually stir in the hot grits.

5. Turn the mixture into the prepared casserole and sprinkle the remaining cheddar and Parmesan and the paprika over the top.

6. Bake in the top third of the oven for 20 to 25 minutes, or until lightly browned. Serve hot.

Variations: Use ½ cup dry white wine in place of the beer and replace the cheddar cheese with Gruyère. Sprinkle with chopped parsley before serving.

Reheat: If at room temperature, reheat at 350°F. for about 25 minutes; if cold, add about 15 minutes.

| Parmesan Spoon Bread |

This light and fluffy casserole "bread" of Southern ancestry is actually somewhere between a savory pudding and a soufflé. It should be served as soon as it is baked, while still puffy. The characteristic crusty top becomes even crustier when sprinkled with Parmesan cheese before baking. After comparing hundreds of recipes for spoonbread I learned that no two are alike. Although most of them require separating the eggs, beating the whites, and then folding them in, after much experimentation I discovered that this is actually an unnecessary step.

MAKES: 6 to 8 side-dish servings
BAKES: At 375°F. for 30 to 40 minutes
CASSEROLE: Generously butter a 1½-quart casserole or ovenproof glass bowl

3 cups milk

¾ cup coarse yellow or white cornmeal

2 tablespoons unsalted butter

¾ teaspoon salt

¼ teaspoon black pepper

3 large eggs

1 cup freshly grated Parmesan cheese (4 ounces)

2 tablespoons all-purpose flour

1 tablespoon baking powder

1. Preheat the oven, and prepare the casserole.
2. Scald 2 cups of the milk in a medium saucepan over moderate heat. In a medium bowl, stir together the cornmeal and the remaining 1 cup milk. Stir

the mixture into the hot milk. Add the butter, salt, and pepper and cook, stirring constantly, until very thick, 4 to 5 minutes.

3. In a large bowl, whisk the eggs until frothy, about 30 seconds. In a small bowl, stir together ¾ cup of the Parmesan with the flour and baking powder. Whisk the mixture into the eggs. Add a large spoonful of the hot cornmeal mixture and whisk to blend. Add the remainder and whisk to blend.

4. Turn the batter into the prepared casserole and sprinkle with the remaining ¼ cup Parmesan.

5. Bake for 30 to 40 minutes, or until puffy and deep golden brown. To serve, spoon out like a soufflé (dividing portions with two spoons, back to back).

Variations: For a South-of-the-Border flavor, replace the Parmesan cheese with grated Mexican *queso cotija* and add ¼ cup chopped cilantro and ½ teaspoon ground cumin to the batter.

Reheat: Not recommended.

| Swiss Cheese Fondue |

This isn't the sort of casserole that you bake, but a communal casserole it is indeed, and one of my favorites. Overexposure of this classic Swiss ritual, during the 1960s, ruined it for many of us. But it is time to reexamine fondue. You really should have a wide, shallow, flameproof casserole called a *Caquelon*, but a chafing dish or enameled cast-iron skillet will do.

MAKES: About 3 cups; 6 side-dish servings

COOKS: At the table

CASSEROLE: Choose a nonreactive, large, shallow, flameproof casserole or chafing dish

2 loaves Swiss peasant bread or crusty farmhouse sourdough bread

1 cup dry white wine

¼ cup kirsch or brandy

1 tablespoon fresh lemon juice

1 tablespoon cornstarch

1½ cups grated Emmentaler cheese (6 ounces)

1½ cups grated Gruyère cheese (6 ounces)

1½ cups grated Fontina cheese (6 ounces)

1 small garlic clove, minced and mashed to a paste with a pinch of salt, or crushed through a press

⅜ teaspoon grated nutmeg

⅛ teaspoon cayenne pepper

½ teaspoon salt

¼ teaspoon black pepper

1. Break the loaves of bread into 3 or 4 large pieces to make them more manageable, and place them in baskets lined with linen napkins. Guests break off pieces as they eat.

2. In the casserole or chafing dish, stir together the wine, kirsch, lemon juice, and cornstarch until blended. Place over low heat and bring to a simmer, stirring constantly. Add the 3 cheeses and the garlic, nutmeg, cayenne, salt, and pepper. Cook, stirring frequently, until smooth, 3 to 4 minutes. Stir vigorously at times so the cheese melts smoothly. The fondue should have a cream-sauce consistency; if necessary, beat in a little wine. Keep the casserole over a small flame while guests dip chunks of bread.

3. Provide guests with long-handled forks so they can spear and dip pieces of bread into the hot fondue. It is important to occasionally stir the fondue during the ritual. Any crusty cheese that forms in the bottom of the pan is called la croûte or la religieuse, and is to be relished by the honored guest, or by all.

Note: The fondue should be stirred frequently during cooking and eating to avoid curdling or burning. If it should begin to curdle, or separate, take the casserole to the kitchen and beat it vigorously over very low heat. If this doesn't repair it, dissolve 1 teaspoon of cornstarch in 1 tablespoon of wine and beat it in. When smooth, return to the flame at the dining table and continue dipping and dining.

Cheese Glossary

Cheeses play an important role in many casseroles. They add fragrance, flavor, texture, and richness while holding layers of ingredients together. They also melt and form mouthwatering golden brown crusty toppings over casseroles. This glossary will give insight to the background and describe the flavors of my favorite cheeses and also suggest options for substituting cheeses.

Asiago: This sensational Italian cheese is becoming increasingly popular and more widely available. Asiago is a hard cheese with a granular (*grana*) texture. Although it is sold mostly as a sharp (aged) cheese, it is also available as mild or medium. Asiago has a pale yellow color and a flavor that seems a cross between a sharp cheddar and an aged Parmesan, but more aromatic. As the cheese ages it becomes harder in consistency, stronger in flavor, and more granular. At four months of age, Asiago has a mild, fresh, clean, buttery flavor with a nutty nuance. Young Asiago is ideal for slicing into wafers. At six months, Asiago becomes firmer, sharper, richer, and nuttier. Aged or sharp Asiago is at least one year old and has a powerful, deep, zesty aroma and flavor, great for grating over pasta. A little goes a long way.
Substitute: Parmesan or romano, perhaps *queso cotija* or *Kephalotyri*.

Blue Cheeses: There are more than fifty varieties of blue-veined cheeses in this general category. Their consistency ranges from soft and creamy to dry and crumbly, with flavor that varies from sweet and tangy to sharp and pungent, though always salty and earthy. The blue veins develop from healthy molds that grow during ripening and add deep flavor. The three biggest blue cheese families are gorgonzola (Italian), Roquefort (French), and Stilton (English). See specific listings for their descriptions. There is a creamy, mild brielike blue cheese worth investigating, called Saga blue. Danish blue and Maytag are excellent sharp and crumbly all-purpose blues.

Substitute: Crumbly blue cheeses are interchangeable. Although there is no exact substitute for creamy young gorgonzola, Saga blue can be used in a pinch.

CHEDDAR: A British creation, cheddar is the most popular cheese in the world. My taste buds must agree, since there are more than twenty recipes in this book calling for cheddar. To many people, cheese *means* cheddar. Cheddar takes its name from the village of Cheddar, in Somerset County, England, and some say that a true cheddar can be made only there.

Cheddar ranges in color from white or creamy to golden, yellow, or bright orange. Color has always been a matter of geographical preference. The coloring of cheddars is contributed by annatto (achiote) seeds, which are also used to color and flavor Caribbean dishes.

English and Canadian cheddars dominate the imported cheddar cheese market, but there are many excellent domestic cheddars to choose from: Wisconsin (including Colby), Oregon Tillamook, New York, Longhorn, Vermont White, and California farmhouse.

There are four main categories of cheddar to choose from, according to age: mild, medium, sharp, and extra-sharp. Cheddar is softest and mildest when young and becomes firmer, more crumbly, sharper, and more complex with age. In general, less cheese is needed when sharp or extra-sharp is used. All cheddars are excellent melting and cooking cheeses.

Mild: At one to three months old, very mild and creamy, even buttery, and most meltable. It is slightly sweet with discernible tangy undertones.

Medium: When three to six months old, distinctively creamy in consistency and beginning to take on its complex flavor. The texture is firm and the flavor is starting to acquire a slight sharpness and tangy richness.

Sharp: After six to ten months, texture begins to take on a crumbly characteristic. Also, with age, the flavor becomes more complex and assumes brothy undertones.

Extra-sharp: Slowly aged for one to two years or longer, crumbly and breaks easily as the elasticity is diminished. The flavor becomes rounder, fuller, sharper, fruitier, and almost beefy. During a recent tasting of precious seven- and eight-year-old cheddars, I noticed a slight crunch to the consistency, and I learned that the calcium in milk begins to precipitate as crunchiness in the pockets. Cheese with bones! This very complex, very sharp cheese flavor remains on your tongue for a long time after tasting.
Substitute: Firm Monterey Jack for mild cheddar.

COTTAGE CHEESE: When acid or rennet is added to warm milk (whole, skim, part skim, and/or buttermilk) and left at room temperature, curds form and separate from the whey (liquid). The curds can be large or small. After being drained in cheesecloth, cottage cheese results. Most cheese making starts out this way. Cottage cheese is bright, creamy white with a fresh tangy milk flavor. It is mild and delicate, rich with butterfat or low in fat, as desired.
Substitute: Ricotta or pot cheese.

CREAM CHEESE: Invented in America around 1880, this creamy white, buttery rich cow's milk cheese tastes best when freshly made. Usually made from a combination of milk and cream, cream cheese melts easily and has a fresh cream flavor. It works beautifully for both sweet and savory dishes. It is most famous as the cheese in cheesecake.
Substitute: Low-fat cream cheese or commercial domestic Neufchâtel, which is quite different from true Neufchâtel.

EMMENTALER: This is the Swiss cheese that is famous for having large holes throughout. Named for the Emme Valley, where it was first created, Emmentaler is one of the most difficult cheeses to make. Temperature is extremely critical through each step of the process, from the heating of the milk (part skim) through the ripening period. Patience is required, too, because the holes, which actually are bubbles of carbon dioxide (as in Champagne or beer), form as the cheese ripens in its own good time. American taste for mild cheese allows Swiss cheese to ripen in sixty days, while four to ten months are required in Switzerland. Emmentaler has a distinct aroma, a firm, dense texture, and evenly spaced holes. The color ranges from pale beige to yellow beige, while the flavor is likened to hazelnuts with a sweet aftertaste. As with most cheeses, the flavor becomes stronger with age.

Swiss cheese melts and cooks beautifully. Excellent Swiss cheeses are imported from Switzerland, Finland, Denmark, and Austria. Wisconsin is the largest producer of domestic Swiss, and Ohio produces excellent ones as well. There are some baby Swiss cheeses on the market; they are soft and silky, mild and buttery, having small eyes and a pale beige color.

Substitute: Jarlsberg or Gruyère.

FETA: The most famous of all Greek cheese, the ancient feta is traditionally made from sheep's milk and sometimes goat's milk. Domestic feta is made from cow's milk. Feta is called a pickled cheese because it is cured in a salty brine. It is chalk-white and crumbly yet creamy, and always salty and tangy. The longer it ripens in its brine, the saltier and sharper it becomes. It is always best to taste a sliver of the feta that you plan to buy. If several are available, taste all of them and compare. Try to buy the freshest. At home, feta will remain freshest if stored in brine (either ask for some at the cheese store or combine half milk and water with a little salt). If not stored in brine, try to use it up within a week. In brine, it should last twice as long. Feta is relatively low in fat compared to many other cheeses (6 grams per ounce as opposed to 9 grams for cheddar). It does not melt; rather, it softens and browns without changing shape. Of the imported fetas, Greek, Bulgarian, Romanian, and French are among the best. Domestic fetas of high quality are being produced in Wisconsin and New York.

Substitute: No real substitute. You can use Bryndza, but that is more difficult to locate than feta.

FONTINA: This elegant, ivory-colored Italian cheese is generally considered to be among the top ten cheeses of the world. It can be made from either cow's milk or sheep's milk. A true Fontina is called Fontina d'Aosta and is made in Piedmont, where people have been making Fontina since the eleventh century. Fontina has a cocoa-brown rind and a waxed veneer. The texture of the cheese is firm and the appearance resembles Gruyère. It has a distinct aroma and a mild, nutty flavor that is not easily categorized. It can be said that

Fontina has the sweet butternut flavor of an aged Emmentaler with the special tang of a good Gruyère, along with a smoky nuance. A superb melting cheese, Fontina is an important component of fondue. Fontina with a red rind is usually blander and more rubbery.

Substitute: Gruyère or half Gruyère and half Swiss Emmentaler.

GORGONZOLA: A marvelous and distinctive blue-veined Italian cheese, gorgonzola is made from whole cow's milk. It has a flavor and consistency that I find addictive. Gorgonzola is available in a variety of ages that range from sweet and creamy with a mild earthy tang to firm or crumbly with a sharp pungency. The flecks of color actually are more green than blue. *Dolce* (sweet) is the name of the young category of gorgonzolas (aged sixty to ninety days), while *piccante* (sharp) gorgonzolas are aged for one year or longer. The best imported gorgonzolas are aged in the grottos and caves of the Valsassina, north of Milan. Gorgonzola is not as sharp as Roquefort. Auricchio, of Wisconsin, makes a sensational domestic gorgonzola that rivals the best imported ones; it is sold under the Bel Gioioso label.

Substitute: Use any crumbly blue for an aged, crumbly gorgonzola. Although there is no perfect substitute for the creamy, young gorgonzola, in a pinch, use Saga blue.

GOUDA: This firm cow's milk cheese from Holland is one of the two most famous Dutch cheeses (the other being Edam). Both date to the Middle Ages. The flavors of the two are similar, but the consistencies differ because of the butterfat content. Gouda is made from whole milk while Edam is made with part skim milk. Because it contains less butterfat, Edam becomes firmer with age. Gouda is richer and softer and has a light, clean, buttery flavor. It is a very dependable, all-purpose cheese, smooth and mellow. Young Gouda (aged two to six months) has a nutty flavor nuance that becomes sharper and tangier when cured longer. Gouda takes well to smoking. When smoked, it has a brown wax rind while other Goudas are coated with a bright yellow rind.

Substitute: Edam for Gouda.

GRUYÈRE: Although originally Swiss, this firm cow's milk cheese is made in both Switzerland and France, in the mountains at the border. Both countries produce superb Gruyères. This is, of course, the cheese used to make quiche lorraine, Swiss fondue, and a multitude of sauces and gratins. Some say that the Swiss Gruyère is a touch sweeter and the French, slightly tangier. Both have a firm texture and nutty flavor, though aging can cancel out the subtleties.

Substitute: Emmentaler or Fontina.

JARLSBERG: This mild Norwegian cheese looks like a Swiss, but doesn't taste like one. Jarlsberg is wide-eyed and firm-textured, with color ranging from creamy white to light yellow. It is buttery, mild, and nutty, an excellent all-purpose cheese for slicing or cooking.

Substitute: Emmentaler or Fontina.

KASSÉRI: Here is a milder, creamier cousin to Greek *Kephalotýri* (made from its reconstituted curds). Some say that the flavor of domestic *Kasséri* is superior to the imported Greek product, with our domestic version tasting somewhat reminiscent of a cross between cheddar and a young Parmesan with a light wine nuance. A young domestic *Kasséri* can be used in place of feta.

Substitute: Romano, Parmesan, or *queso cotija*.

KEPHALOTÝRI (KEFALOTIRI): Named for the head shape that it resembles, this hard Greek cheese is made from sheep's milk or goat's milk. In Greece, you can find young *Kephalotýri*, which is good for slicing and eating out of hand; here, usually just the aged variety is available. It is yellowish in color, sharp and pungent, hard enough for grating, and always salty.

Substitute: Romano, Parmesan, or *queso cotija*.

MONTEREY JACK: Also called Monterey or Jack for short, this semisoft cow's milk cheese was invented in Monterey, California, around 1892. It is a distant cousin of cheddar and a variation on domestic Muenster. Monterey Jack has a high moisture content and is an excellent melting cheese. Tex-Mex and Southwestern cookery (which often combine it with cheddar) would be at a loss without it. Most commonly available as a young and mild cheese (just three to six weeks old), it can, however, be aged, becoming firmer in texture

and stronger in flavor. The mild version is delicate and buttery with a slight tang and creamy consistency. Dry Jack or dry Monterey can be found; it has been aged for six months or more and is hard enough for grating.
Substitute: Muenster, Havarti, or mild cheddar.

MOZZARELLA: This quintessential Italian "pizza cheese" was originally made from rich and creamy water buffalo milk (*mozzarella di bufala*). Nowadays it is mostly made from cow's milk (whole or skim). There are two basic types of mozzarella cheese: fresh (stored in water) and slightly aged up to two months; and vacuum-packed in plastic. Fresh mozzarella is white and has a soft, spongy texture and sweet buttery flavor. It is available salted or unsalted. Most agree that fresh mozzarella tastes best when eaten within hours of making, before giving it a chance to chill. The slightly aged cream-colored variety of mozzarella is firmer and more elastic. It is the type most frequently found in supermarkets and has a much longer shelf life than fresh mozzarella.

Because *mozzarella di bufala* is richer in butterfat than cow's milk mozzarella, I sometimes marinate sliced or grated cow's milk mozzarella in a little olive oil and it becomes more tender.
Substitute: String cheese or mild provolone for slightly aged mozzarella or, in a pinch, Monterey Jack or Muenster. There is no substitute for fresh mozzarella. Of course, cow's milk mozzarella can be substituted for *mozzarella di bufala*.

MUENSTER: Originally made in Alsace, France, this mild, creamy semisoft cow's milk cheese has an orange or white surface. At six to eight weeks, it is very mild, creamy, and buttery. At three months, it becomes creamier, smoother, and more pungent. It is an excellent melting cheese.
Substitute: Monterey Jack or Havarti.

PARMESAN: The very best imported Parmesan is labeled *Parmigiano Reggiano* and has been aged for at least eighteen months. When buying a wedge, check for the words "Parmigiano Reggiano" tattooed on the rind. Good Parmesan cheese should be a pale golden straw color and have the fresh fragrance of a grassy meadow on a rainy day. It will have a hard granular consistency but won't be overly dry. Parmesan is most often finely grated, as needed, to release its mouthwatering aroma, but it is also perfect for slicing into paper-thin wafers. The sophisticated flavor of Parmesan will be deep and complex, with both buttery and nutty dimensions and a certain saltiness. It should be sharp but offer no bitter aftertaste.

The art of producing Parmesan in and around Parma is very serious business, and great care is taken from the start, from fresh green grazing pastures, to nourished happy cows, to production, storage, handling, maturing, and eating. Parmigiano Reggiano can be made only during certain times of the year, when the milk is at its richest. Needless to say, all of this care adds to the cost of this precious cheese.

To store a wedge of Parmesan, wrap it in several layers of damp cheese-cloth or paper towels, then put it in a plastic bag and store it in the refrigerator. Unwrap, grate, or slice and rewrap as you use it.

Younger domestic Parmesan is available and can be used as a substitute for the Parmesan, but it will lack a certain complexity and authority. I predict that this will change in the future and that well-aged domestic Parmesan will be available.

Substitute: Romano, Asiago, *queso cotija*, or *Kephalotýri*.

PEPATO: When Sicilian pecorino romano is richly studded with whole black peppercorns, it becomes Pepato. Not only does the pepper contribute tremendous flavor but it gives the cheese a beautiful appearance. Pepato is best sliced into wafers for serving or grated and used in cooking. Pepato has all the qualities of romano, but with the surprise of a peppery crunch. My favorite domestic version is made by Casaro in Wisconsin.

Substitute: Romano or Parmesan mixed with a little coarse black pepper.

PROVOLONE: Made from whole cow's milk, this aromatic, full-flavored Italian cheese is available in mild, medium, and sharp, depending on age. The color of provolone will be creamy white to pale beige. Texture will range from semisoft to hard. Even the mildest provolone will have a certain strength and authority all its own, with a sweet, nutty nuance. Medium provolone will be firmer and more pronounced in aroma and flavor. Aged provolone is much stronger, sharper, and very aromatic. With aging the consistency becomes more granular and the flavor becomes fuller.

Provolones are often shaped into balls (and sometimes fanciful shapes like pigs or cows), dipped into a golden wax coating, and tied with cord and hung. Sometimes provolone are smoked.

Substitute: Aged mozzarella; a firm Monterey Jack can be used in place of a mild provolone.

QUESO COTIJA: A hard, aged Mexican cheese with a creamy white color and pungent aroma, *queso cotija* has a dry, granular consistency. It can be finely crumbled or grated. With its sharp robust flavor, saltiness, and slight acidity, *queso cotija* gives an air of south-of-the-border authenticity to tacos, enchiladas, beans, and tortilla casseroles. Wrapped in plastic, it will keep well for six months to a year.

Substitute: Romano, Parmesan, or *Kephalotýri*.

RICOTTA: Wonderfully rich and creamy, fresh ricotta is familiar to all of us who love lasagne and other cheese-stuffed pastas. It is a cousin to cottage cheese, though always made with acidity to separate the curds and whey, rather than with rennet; the result is a sweet, creamy milk flavor, since there is no fermentation. This quality makes ricotta suitable for both sweet and savory preparations, from cannoli to cannelloni. The curds are small, giving ricotta its familiar grainy consistency. You can buy it fresh in bulk from good Italian markets or in plastic cartons from the supermarket. The degree of rich-ness will vary depending on whether it was made from whole milk, skim milk, or a combination. There is also a hard, dry aged ricotta, called ricotta salata, for grating.

Substitute: Well-drained small-curd cottage cheese, pureed in the food processor, if desired.

ROMANO: The classic romano cheese is actually called pecorino romano, meaning that it was made from sheep's milk. Also available are vacchino romano, made from cow's milk, and caprino romano, made from goat's milk. They are all hard grating cheeses with a strong aroma and sharp, salty, robust flavor. Romano does not have the sophisticated flavor subtleties of a good Parmesan, so it stands up well to other strong flavors like anchovies and cured olives. The older the cheese, the harder and sharper it will be. A good

pecorino romano is aged at least six months. Cow's milk romanos (including domestic romanos) are milder than the others.
Substitute: Parmesan, locatelli, *Kephalotýri*, or *queso cotija*.

ROQUEFORT: Called the "king of blues" since it was created in the caves of Roquefort, France, during the first century A.D., this blue-veined cheese has a strong aroma and a semisoft, creamy-crumbly consistency. The pungent flavor and saltiness intensify as the cheese ripens in the caves of Roquefort, where the good mold, *Penicillium roqueforti*, was first discovered.
Substitute: Any other sharp crumbly cheese.

STILTON: This magnificent British blue cheese is firm and slightly crumbly. It has a complex, sophisticated flavor that is milder and tamer than Roquefort or a well-aged gorgonzola, though assertive enough on its own.
Substitute: Any sharp crumbly blue cheese.

SWISS CHEESE: This general term applies to all of the Emmentaler cheeses with large eyes. See individual listings for description.
Substitute: Any domestic or imported Swiss or Emmentaler, or Jarlsberg.

Acknowledgments

I give special heartfelt thanks to all those who helped with bringing this book to life.

Lenny Allen

Amy Boorstein

Roger Bourget

Michael Carlisle

Tina Constable

Brown Cranna

Joan Denman

Cathy and Rus DePriest

Charles DiCagno

Roy Finamore

Airi Fobel

Linda Funk

Patrick Geoghegan

Rowann Gilman

Jennifer Graff

Marcella Hazan

Anna Mae Hubert

Steve Jenkins

Michael Kalmen

Paul Kergoat

Kathleen Holmgren Krichmar

Jere Kupecky

Reid Larrance

M. A. McQuade

Jim Paltridge

Peter Prestcott

Dr. Robert W. Ramsey

Mardee and Gary Regan

Maddie Shevlin

Bob and Bernadette Simms

Astrid Sinkler

Renato Stanisic

Carol and David Stenroos

Jonathan Stuart

Diana Sturgis

Paul Sylvester

John Thomas

Myra Wahlstrom

Index

Conversion Chart

Equivalent Imperial and Metric Measurements

American cooks use standard containers, the 8-ounce cup and a tablespoon that takes exactly 16 level fillings to fill that cup level. Measuring by cup makes it very difficult to give weight equivalents, as a cup of densely packed butter will weigh considerably more than a cup of flour. The easiest way therefore to deal with cup measurements in recipes is to take the amount by volume rather than by weight. Thus the equation reads:

1 cup =240 ml =8 fl. oz.
½ cup =120 ml =4 fl. oz.

It is possible to buy a set of American cup measures in major stores around the world.

In the States, butter is often measured in sticks. One stick is the equivalent of 8 tablespoons. One tablespoon of butter is therefore the equivalent to ¹/₂ ounce/15 grams.

Solid Measures

U.S. and Imperial Measures		Metric Measures	
Ounces	Pounds	Grams	Kilos
1		28	
2		56	
3¹/₂		100	
4	¹/₄	112	
5		140	
6		168	
8	¹/₂	225	
9		250	¹/₄
12	³/₄	340	
16	1	450	
18		500	¹/₂
20	1¹/₄	560	
24	1¹/₂	675	
27		750	³/₄
32	2	900	
36	2¹/₄	1000	1

Oven Temperature Equivalents

Fahrenheit	Celsius	Gas Mark	Description
225	110	¹/₄	Cool
250	130	¹/₂	
275	140	1	Very Slow
300	150	2	
325	170	3	Slow
350	180	4	Moderate
375	190	5	
400	200	6	Moderately Hot
425	220	7	Fairly Hot
450	230	8	Hot
475	240	9	Very Hot
500	250	10	Extremely Hot

Liquid Measures

Fluid Ounces	U.S.	Imperial	Milliliters
	1 teaspoon	1 teaspoon	5
¹/₄	2 teaspoons	1 dessertspoon	10
¹/₂	1 tablespoon	1 tablespoon	14
1	2 tablespoons	2 tablespoons	28
2	¹/₄ cup	4 tablespoons	56
4	¹/₂ cup		110
5		¹/₄ pint/1 gill	140
6	³/₄ cup		170
8	1 cup		225
9			250, ¹/₄ liter
10	1¹/₄ cups	¹/₂ pint	280
15		³/₄ pint	420
16	2 cups		450
18	2¹/₄ cups		500, ¹/₂ liter
20	2¹/₂ cups	1 pint	560
24	3 cups		675
25		1¹/₄ pints	700
27	3¹/₂ cups		750
30	3³/₄ cups	1¹/₂ pints	840
32	4 cups or 1 quart		900
36	4¹/₂ cups		1000, 1 liter
40	5 cups	2 pints/1 quart	1120